MW00478358

Mo ving i ast
Mediocre

Unlocking Your Mind to Create the Life You've
Always Imagined

Nick Matiash

363 PRESS

Moving Past Mediocre / Nick Matiash. -- 1st ed.

ISBN 978-1-7330246-1-7 (pbk)

ISBN 978-1-7330246-0-0 (eBook)

Cover design by JetLaunch

www.MovingPastMediocre.com

To my beautiful, loving, supportive wife, Christina:

This book is for you. Everything in these pages was born out of the rabbit hole that your love sent me down. I am who I am because of the man that I desired to be for you, for Lucy, and for any future children that we're blessed with. I will never be able to thank you enough for being you, and for allowing me to be me. You're my favorite human.

CONTENTS

Nobody ever aims to be average. It's not a favorable title to own, but so many of us slide into it with ease. Sometimes—oftentimes—mediocrity is *just* comfortable enough to keep your feet firmly planted where you'd rather they not be.

"Eh, that exciting life I've been dreaming about can wait until tomorrow. A new season of The Ranch *just uploaded on Netflix, so I'm booked for the next few hours."*

After sinking into your couch for a couple of episodes of not-that-funny TV, the bright lights of the life that previously excited you have all but turned off. *Damn you, Ashton.*

Even though no one in his right mind aspires to climb the ladder of success and stop firmly in the middle, the vast majority of us tend to set up shop right around that point. Why is that? No one has hopes and dreams to live in the middle of the pack, yet we tend to do just enough to land there. And when we do, we're simultaneously grateful that life isn't so bad and bitter that it isn't better.

Sounds like a bummer, right? To say that life is good and, in the same moment, believe that it hasn't played out the way you'd like it to is sort of baffling. You become a living, breathing contradiction.

That's where I found myself a little over five years ago.

I was teaching math at a school that sucked the life out of me, but it was a steady paycheck. I was in a relationship that I wasn't fulfilled by, but we'd been together for four and a half years, she wasn't a terrible human, and I wasn't getting any younger (at the time, I was apparently a naive twenty-four-year-old mentally going on forty-five). I wasn't broke, but I wasn't rich. I wasn't unhappy, but I wasn't in love with my life. I wasn't fat, but I wasn't exactly in shape.

You get the picture. My life was pretty *meh*.

I was mediocrity personified. And, to make it worse, I knew it. I felt it in my bones. I felt the days, weeks, and months pass by and just hoped that at some point I would be able to snap out of it.

Luckily, I did. Otherwise writing this book would be a bit of a sham, right?

All it took was a breakup, letting go of what I thought I wanted and needed, and a chance meeting with a gorgeous girl about a month after I had cut ties with my ex. Well, all that plus a lot of intentional work on myself once I figured out that my life was mine to create.

So, where am I now?

I am happily married to a beautiful woman who is *definitely* out of my league. We just had our first kid, a little girl named Lucy. I'm not exactly a bodybuilder, but I'm in pretty great shape. I'm still teaching math, but at a great school in the town where we just bought a house. On top of teaching math, I'm a writer and life coach, helping others shake the funk that I once found myself in.

In short: *I fucking love my life.*

I don't have millions of dollars, a big-ass boat, or the funds necessary to travel the world on a whim. But I've figured out how to smile more and frown less. I've learned how to focus on things I can control and let go of things I can't. I've become more focused on all that I do have rather than lamenting the things that I don't. Life is good over here.

This book is for anyone who may find themselves camping out halfway up the ladder of their version of success. It's a shitty place to be. Yes, it could be worse—you could be terminally ill, unemployed, or hopelessly lost in all of your most important relationships.

But it could also be better.

Way better than you've imagined it could be. At this very moment, you can dream only as big as your capacity to understand what's possible for you. That imagination is limited by your life experiences and what you've observed in close proximity to you.

I'm here to help you widen the scope of what's possible. Your logical brain won't be happy with us at first, but I promise it will be worth it.

My mission is to show you everything I know about how to make the remaining years of your life better, more fulfilling, more loving, and more abundant. I don't have all the answers, but I've come up with some of them, and you'll read them over in the next couple hundred pages or so.

One thing I'll say before we get rocking here is, in order for the following chapters to give you the most value, you need to embrace the concepts wholeheartedly. If you approach everything you come across with a tinge of, "Well this is some bullshit," you'll be wasting your time, money, and energy. I don't want that for you, and you shouldn't want it for yourself.

Honor your time. Honor the money you spent on this book. Honor the energy you are bringing to each page. You can't get where you want to go by judging every step of the path with your arms folded across your chest. You have to be open to letting new ideas spend some time in that brain of yours. Let them play around and see if they stick.

These ideas will only make a difference if you allow them to. Let 'em in.

ONE MORE QUICK NOTE

I don't want this book and the information within it to sit on your mental shelf and start collecting dust the minute you finish reading it. By clicking on this link, you'll be inducted into the exclusive Facebook group where these ideas will come to life—Moving Past Mediocre: The Community.

This community will be a place for you to ask questions about what you've read, share insights from what you've learned, and interact with amazing people like yourself who have read the content you're about to dig into.

Join the group now, or wait until you get further along in the journey. Just know that we'll be there when you're ready to continue the discussion that begins on the next page. Enjoy!

Chapter 1

Does Life Really Begin at the End of Your Comfort Zone?

When my wife, Christina, and I started dating, I jokingly made the bold claim that I had come up with the phrase, "Your life begins at the end of your comfort zone." I told her that I received royalties when other people used it and that I chose to stay anonymous to avoid the public eye. I'm pretty sure she was playing along for my benefit as she laughed, because she has admitted since then that I'm not her brand of funny. Don't get me wrong, she loves me very much. She just prefers comedy that doesn't lean on dad jokes so heavily.

Where was I? Ah right, the comfort zone thing.

I've always found it interesting that I chose that particular quote to fake brag about when we were courting each other. In hindsight, my trajectory from then to now seems to align well with the words that a guy not named Nick Matiash came up with (Neale Donald Walsch, for those who are studying for an upcoming stint on *Jeopardy*).

My life as I know it—life coach, content creator, and man with an endless thirst for getting better—started when I met Christina. And as you may have guessed, pursuing her was, in fact, out of my comfort zone. I had just ended a four-and-a-half-year relationship and had told anyone who would listen that I was ready to enjoy the single life. There was also the fact that she lived an hour and a half away from me. In my mind, dating a girl within ten miles wasn't to be entertained, so 100 miles sounded comical in comparison. And yet, there I was, chasing down this girl from another area code, beginning the life that has led me here.

But this chapter isn't about me waxing poetic about my wife or our love story (did I mention we met on a freaking elevator?). It's about how most people confuse the message of the quote I used to take credit for.

Comfort zones aren't the enemy here. Familiar zones are.

When most people talk about doing something outside of their comfort zone, they are likely referring to something that makes them uncomfortable. Maybe it's finally calling up that girl and asking her on a date. Maybe it's joining that Crossfit gym that you've been eyeing for months. Maybe it's asking your boss for a promotion. There are plenty of things you could likely add to the list of things that make you uncomfortable, hence putting you outside of your comfort zone.

And, if all of these examples make you uncomfortable, it would make sense that their opposites be deemed comfortable, right? Let's play this out for a second before we decide.

The opposite of calling up that girl and asking her out would be not calling her, staying in, and spending the night potentially alone. The opposite of joining that Crossfit gym is recommitting to your couch and doubling down on your expanding waistline. The opposite of asking your boss for that promotion is sitting in your office silently resenting the guy who had the balls to ask for it, got it, and is now making $10,000 more than you will this year.

So, what was presumed to be "comfort zone" actions—not asking her out, not joining the gym, not asking for a promotion—have left you lonely, chubby, and wanting to drink in the middle of the workday.

What part of that sounds comfortable to you?

It's a nightmare, if you ask me.

But I see this all the time, both with my clients and with people I interact with on the day-to-day. They hold on to the mantra of, "I just gotta do more things outside of my comfort zone," all while continuing to do things that don't make them comfortable at all. They're *already* outside a zone of comfort, stuck in a zone of familiarity.

Being 100 pounds overweight isn't comfortable, but it's an identity and lifestyle that people grow accustomed to. The familiarity is what makes it hard to change, not the comfort of the situation.

An abusive relationship—physical, mental, or emotional—is the furthest thing from a comfortable circumstance. But people stay because they know their partner, are scared of the alternative (loneliness), and don't know any other way. Familiarity 101.

Being broke wouldn't be qualified as comfortable by many people either. But once you get used to paying your bills late, living in rough neighborhoods, and eating McDonalds for dinner most nights, those habits become easier than overhauling your life and habits to make more of yourself.

Comfort is NOT the enemy; what's familiar to you is. Familiarity will win every time if you aren't careful. And here's why.

Familiar vs. Fear of the Unknown

The opposite of what is familiar to you would be what is unfamiliar, yes? The unfamiliar is the unknown, and the unknown has been terrifying you since you were a little kid.

Remember the boogeyman? Has anyone ever met him? If you have, get in touch with me because I would love to learn more about this mysterious fella.

The boogeyman's power resided in our fear of what might be under the bed, in our closet, or in the basement. There was no physical evidence of this guy hanging around the house. There was only the story that we created in our heads about how big, scary, and menacing this make-believe creature was. He is the personification of the unknown. We were petrified to get out of bed to go to the bathroom in the middle of the night because we feared getting snatched up by him.

"Is he out there? Is he not? I don't know!" As a result of our cowardice to challenge the unknown of the dark bedroom and the hallway between us and the bathroom, what happened?

We pissed ourselves.

And now, some of us are metaphorically pissing ourselves as adults. The fear of the unknown is real, and it's one of the biggest reasons people never change. This is why familiarity so often wins. We get all hyped up and high on our readiness to make a positive shift in life and then look out into the abyss of the unknown and decide that it's probably better (read: safer) where we are.

It's why I waited four and a half years to break it off with the girl I dated in my early twenties. I knew in my gut that I wasn't going to marry her—willfully, anyway—well before we actually ended things. But I stayed and continued to stare out into the abyss of the unknown. What if no one ever loved me again? What if it's the biggest mistake of my life? What if my next relationship's even worse? Trying to answer those questions were the Boogeyman's brand of scary, so I stuck around and symbolically pissed myself for a while.

> NOTHING KEEPS YOU STUCK MORE THAN YOUR PERCEPTION THAT IF YOU WERE TO MOVE FORWARD AND TAKE ON THE UNKNOWN, YOU WILL ONLY FIND SOMETHING WORSE THAN WHAT YOU CURRENTLY HAVE.

You may have had the same approach with an old job, relationship, or some other milestone moment in your life. You knew you were hanging onto something that no longer did anything for you. But, as you looked out at what might be waiting for you in the unknown, the fear that sent a chill down your spine was much colder than that lukewarm feeling that familiarity gave you.

I've got some news for you though my friends. Different does not equal worse. Trust me.

DIFFERENT NEVER HAS TO EQUAL WORSE

There's an underlying issue with our crippling fear of the unknown: **within that fear is a baked-in belief that if something changes or is different from the way it is now, it is inherently worse.**

You recognize how messed up that is, right? The idea that every time you work up the nerve to do something differently, your mind defaults to, *"Hey man, that's probably going to make your life worse than it already is."*

If you haven't exercised in years, your brain will find a way to convince you that it might not be a good idea to get back at it.

"What if you hurt yourself? What if you embarrass yourself? What if you lose all this weight and gain it all back again? That would suck. It's probably best if you just make another bowl of popcorn and deepen that dent in the couch. It's safe there."

You probably don't have this thought pattern consciously, but it's still happening. All of that chatter that guides you back to your couch is occurring in your subconscious mind. But unfortunately, your subconscious mind is drunk sometimes.

Drunk with good intentions, but drunk nonetheless.

You see, your subconscious mind will always look for the safest bet, the thing that will do you the least harm. This was really helpful back in the days when your ancestors were kicking it with hungry animals twice their size out in the wild. Back then, the subconscious mind was a godsend and is probably the reason why you're here, reading this book. Your great-great-great-great-great granddaddy was once out on the hunt and innately knew that a wild beast was lurking. His subconscious mind clued him in to the impending danger and helped him get the heck out of there without making him consciously sit down and weigh the pros and cons of sticking around to face the animal that would tear him to shreds. It kept him safe without making him use his conscious mind to work it all out for himself.

Some things change, yet some things stay the same. It's been quite some time since we needed that kind of protection from the dangerous environment around us, but here we are with the same subconscious mind that loves itself some safety.

Going to the gym won't threaten your life in any serious way. But it will threaten your weak knees. It will threaten your ego. It will threaten your identity. It will threaten your self-esteem. And since your subconscious mind is hellbent on making you feel safe, it gently guides you back to the couch with a beer in your hand. "The gym is just too different from your normal routine and what you're familiar with. You should kick your feet up and relax," says the ever-present subconscious mind.

Different is scary. Different feels unsafe. And, to your previously heroic subconscious mind, different sounds a lot worse than the status quo of what's currently going on. Different doesn't have to be worse, though. That's just our mind playing tricks on us. So we sit, waiting for our life to change for the better while at the same time refusing to try anything different. I'm sure I don't have to tell you that this isn't the best formula for positive transformation.

> COURAGE AND FEAR ARE NOT MUTUALLY EXCLUSIVE--YOU USUALLY DON'T SEE ONE WITHOUT THE OTHER. BEING AFRAID DOESN'T EXCUSE YOU FROM GOING FOR MORE; IT'S A SIGN THAT YOU NEED TO BUCK UP AND DO IT.

There are plenty of people out there who have pushed back against their subconscious mind, fought through what's familiar, and truly moved past mediocre. The rest of this book is going to show you how to do the same. I needed to start here so that you would know what you were up against.

What's familiar to you is keeping you stuck in mediocrity, and your subconscious mind is sitting in the driver's seat of that road trip, ordering up the same directions and the same destinations over and over again.

It's time you took back the wheel, don't you think?

PART 1

The Subconscious:
The Gifts and the Curses

Alright, I just spent a few pages hating on the sub-conscious mind and its role in keeping you stuck, but it's not always out to get you. It has its perks, too.

It allows you to brush your teeth without calculating the correct angle at which you should be hitting those incisors. It assists you on your commute to work so that you don't have to ponder each turn, exit, and lane change. It even helps you read this or any other book without having to donate any mental power to keeping your heart beating. Wouldn't it be something if you had to plan for and execute every beat of your heart? Your brain would be pretty tapped out if you had to keep track of all that. So, yes, your subconscious mind isn't 100 percent evil. It truly is a gift—but you have to truly understand it to get the most out of it. If you don't, you'll just be at the mercy of whatever it wants to do with you. And that's what this first section is all about.

We're going to pull back the curtain on the guy who's really at the control board of your mind and learn how to harness his potential. Once you see your subconscious for the beauty and beast that it is, you'll be able to take full advantage of its wizardry.

You've got a lot of stuff bubbling beneath the surface of what you consciously understand and are able to use. Once you bring it out into the open, you'll wonder how you ever lived your life without such awareness and power.

Let's dive into the deep, deep waters of the subconscious mind...

Chapter 2

Autopilot You

August 26th, 2004 may have been a normal day for you, but it was a day that I had anticipated for years. When I went to bed the night before, I was merely an insignificant fifteen-year-old. When my eyes opened that day as a freshly minted 16-year-old, I was legally allowed to get behind the wheel of a car and drive—provided I passed the test to get my permit, anyway.

I woke up feeling all sorts of excited, as I knew my mom would be taking me over to the DMV bright and early. I wasn't big on studying back in those days, so I probably used the ten-minute car ride to read through the little study booklet as quickly as I could. Most kids would read over that thing for weeks leading up to their hopeful induction into the world of driving, but I chose to sift through the bold and italicized words on the way to take the test and see what would stick.

From my recollection, I missed one question. There was some road sign that I didn't recognize, and it ruined my perfect score. Don't worry, it wasn't a stop sign or anything. All I knew was that I passed.

"I can drive now (with an adult in the passenger seat, of course)."

My mom decided to drive home and told me that I could get some practice later on a few of the streets by our house that weren't as busy as the ones we were about to travel on. It seemed like a good enough plan, so I hopped in the passenger seat and smiled all the way home. I'm sure I just sat around for the rest of the day daydreaming, thinking about the many destinations I would seek out once I got behind the wheel.

Later that night I had hockey practice, and my dad was set to accompany me, as he usually did. Before we left for the rink, he turned to me and asked, "Hey, did you want to drive?" Excitement (with a side of fear) ran through me as I smiled and agreed to his offer. I settled into the driver's seat, buckled up, and turned the key to hear the sweet sound of the engine. It was "go" time.

I didn't roll to the smoothest stops at each corner, and most of my turns were awkward and jagged, but they kept us safely in the middle of the road. When we hit the expressway, however, things got a little dicey. Since it was my first time behind the wheel, I had never changed lanes while traveling at 65 mph.

I turned my head to look over my shoulder, and the wheel must've turned with it. I found myself in the middle of the lane I had planned to merge into gracefully. There was little to no grace involved as my dad leapt over to straighten the wheel while I was still peeking backwards.

Once I settled into the lane I wanted to be in, things didn't get much better. I had on big, heavy boots that pushed the gas pedal to the floor with ease. I looked up and saw 80 mph on the speedometer.

"Oh shit. Do I brake in the middle of the highway? Do I just let off the gas? Do I just take my hands off of the wheel and hope that my dad can take over?"

I knew it was bad when he quickly hung up with a friend who he was on the phone with in order to talk me down. We eventually made it to practice without incident, but I definitely gave my dad a few more grays on the way.

The best part? My dad had no idea that it was my first time behind the wheel. He assumed I drove home with my mom after getting my permit and got a taste for some of the subtleties of steering, braking, and changing lanes. Negative. I couldn't have been less experienced. But hey, we made it out alive.

If I were to hop in a car and start up the engine today, I wouldn't feel the excitement and nervousness that struck me back then. In fact, I probably wouldn't feel anything. Driving doesn't incite panic, excitement, or nervousness when you've done it thousands and thousands of times. But the lack of excitement pales in comparison to the lack of conscious thought that occurs when I hop in the driver's seat. I could listen to some music, talk to my wife in the passenger seat, and wave at my daughter in the rearview mirror while she smiles from her car seat--all while making it from Point A to Point B without a conscious thought about each turn, lane change, and exit that needs to be taken.

My thoughts and emotions have no place in the act of driving anymore, but back on August 26th, 2004, these systems were overloaded with information and input as I tried to drive for the first time. I couldn't keep up with all the actions I needed to take, thoughts I needed to think, and maneuvers I needed to make. Today, my conscious mind takes a nap in between my driveway and my destination.

I know you've been there, too. You leave work in a fog, put on your favorite Spotify playlist to decompress, and suddenly you're in your driveway. You weren't fully conscious as every yellow light turned red or every person slammed on their brakes in front of you. You just reacted and got yourself home without being consciously aware of anything, really.

And for some reason that doesn't freak any of us out. We just accept this zombie-like, autopilot state for what it is, as long as it keeps getting us home safely. But since we've driven a car so many times, our subconscious mind doesn't need the instructional manual anymore. It's fine on its own, even if we don't check in with it along the way.

THE LAND OF HABITS

Driving isn't the only thing in life that evolves from a taxing experience to an afterthought. There are plenty of activities that you've likely engaged with repeatedly, to the point that they're now second nature. For instance, when was the last time you thought about walking? Not speed walking for exercise or anything like that; just *walking*. Your brain doesn't have to fire up its engines for you to take step after step after step throughout your day, but there was a time when taking those steps consumed every molecule in your skull. The sheer focus on a baby's face as they inch their foot out into the unknown of the next shaky step is something to behold. Now, you just casually stride, one foot in front of the other, until you get where you need to go. No sweat.

I mentioned before that your subconscious mind has some beauty along with some beast. The beautiful side shows up with these downloaded processes of driving, walking, and anything else that you no longer have to think about mid-task. There are so many things that you once struggled with, or at least dedicated a *lot* of thought to. Brushing your teeth, writing your name, navigating your smartphone, changing a diaper, dancing...the list could go on forever.

What happens is that these activities begin on the conscious side of the fence, but after a while they jump that fence and start hanging out in your subconscious—the Land of Habits. Once something becomes habitual—whether it be tying your shoes or playing guitar—you use less and less mental energy to complete the task. You don't require as much focus or concentration once you've crossed into your subconscious where all of your habits reside.

The acts of cooking, reading, getting dressed, and whipping up the perfect cup of coffee all live in this Land of Habits. You know how people say, "Oh, I just don't pay it any mind"? That's literally what your subconscious mind is there for. You don't have to *spend* any conscious mental energy on the automatic behaviors that your subconscious mind can handle. You pay little to no attention to what you're doing, and yet you still manage to get by as a human.

WOULDN'T IT BE AWESOME TO
"PAY NO MIND" TO THINGS LIKE
MAKING MONEY, FINDING LOVE,
OR GETTING SHREDDED?
IT'S NOT ONLY POSSIBLE BUT
PROBABLE...ONCE YOU GET YOUR
SUBCONSCIOUS ONBOARD,
ANYWAY.

Again, this is the beauty of the subconscious side of your mind. It takes things that you have done repeatedly and simply memorizes the program. Once those habitual patterns are imprinted on your subconscious, you don't have to do much at all to get through the tasks that you consistently engage in.

Pretty awesome, right? I mean, it would be a pain if you had to contemplate every step you took, sound out every word you read, and think through every moment of your day. So for that, we can offer some sincere gratitude to our friend, the subconscious mind.

HABITS AREN'T JUST ACTIONS

Here's where the water gets a little murky. Putting your ability to drive, read, or write on autopilot is pretty cool, but those are all actions. Habits are simply repeated patterns, and since we live in a world of action, we tend to see habits through the lens of repeated action. But habits can also be repeated patterns of thought, emotion, and mindset. And since all of those things are intangible, it's hard to see what unseen habitual patterns are good and which are bad.

Actions live in the daylight; beliefs, emotions, and thought patterns live in the dark. You can clearly see if you've developed some bad habits, like eating too many Oreos at night or drinking too much booze during the workday. Even though those actions are the work of your subconscious mind, you can consciously see the result of what's going on and then decide to do something differently. When you can see it with your own two eyes, it's easier to switch things up.

*"Alright, it's time I got my shit together. No whiskey until **after** lunch."*

Thoughts, emotions, and beliefs, however, live below the surface and can go unchecked for years. You can wake up at thirty and believe something that was imprinted on your brain when you were eight years old without ever before knowing it was there. And, if that thought or belief had a negative connotation while running on a constant loop for a couple of decades, you might find yourself in a rut that you can't find your way out of—yet have no idea why.

Imagine if you had a bad habit of devouring an entire large pizza before bed every night, and did that for two straight decades. Don't you think that might cause some issues for your physical wellbeing? Now imagine that you repeated thoughts like, "No one loves me," or "I'm a loser," for two decades. Do you think that could affect your emotional wellbeing? Of course it would! But since emotions and thoughts of the subconscious mind bubble below the surface, it's harder for us to pinpoint what needs adjusting. It's easy to see that you should ditch the pizza, but the negative self-talk? Not so much.

Your subconscious thoughts, emotions, and beliefs are all just kind of hiding in the bushes, waiting to pop out whenever the time is right. You can't see them, but you sense that they're there. Maybe you have negative thoughts that you've had for years and have never revisited. Maybe an event triggered an emotion way back when, and whenever something similar happens in your life, the emotion rises to the surface, seemingly out of nowhere. Maybe your parents passed on some belief about money, race, or politics that you just accepted as truth.

No matter what the thought is, if it's been running on repeat in your mind without your awareness, it will continue to do so until you identify it and do something about it. You've made a habit out of acting, thinking, and feeling in a certain way for a very long time. You've been on autopilot for far too long. Exactly how long? Longer than you think.

Chapter 3

The Buffalo Bills and Your Subconscious Beliefs

The Buffalo Bills are mediocre at best. Maybe if they read this book, they can move past it…

I'm starting to see why my wife doesn't think I'm funny.

Anyway, the Bills have been hard to watch for most of my life. I grew up in Niagara Falls, NY, twenty or thirty minutes from Buffalo. Just about everyone in the area—from diapers to Depends—is a Bills fans, despite the fact that they missed out on the playoffs for seventeen straight seasons (a streak they *finally* broke in late 2017). I always thought it was strange that there's such a dedicated fanbase for a team that looks like they play hungover most Sunday afternoons.

To truly understand the passionate members of the #BillsMafia, you would need to step into a time machine. One of the biggest reasons so many people bleed blue and red for their beloved Bills was their streak of Super Bowl appearances in the early 1990s. From 1991-1994, the Buffalo Bills made a habit of getting to the championship game every year. They also made a habit of finishing each of those years in second place. In those days, each and every Bills fan would joyously celebrate yet another trip to the Super Bowl, only to be let down by another crushing defeat. It was quite the cocktail of hope and despair over the course of those four years, I would imagine. Despite the Super Bowl losses, being the best team in your conference for four straight years is still pretty impressive.

I was alive at the time, but I don't consciously remember much about it. I was only about three years old when they began their run as the runner up, so I don't really recall any of it. But if you listen to some of the biggest Bills fans tell their stories of that golden era, you will hear poetry in their words. The early 90s are spoken about with such reverence by those who witnessed them in real time. I'm sure it was an awesome time to be a Bills fan. Any team that puts together a hot streak like that will definitely make things exciting. And with that, I also understand that the residue of that excitement could last lifetimes, so I bear no judgment on the people who were alive and well to experience the four straight years of quality Bills football.

But, what baffles me is the adoring fanhood that my millennial brethren bestow upon the present day roster of the Buffalo Bills. Most of us never (consciously) witnessed the hot streak that the early 90s produced, yet some of my friends and family stay true to the boys in red and blue. Between 2000 and 2017, the Bills won more games than they lost only *three times*. In seventeen years! Three times! But the parking lot is full of happy tailgaters every Sunday morning.

How could a team that has had such a lackluster twenty years have a raving fan base of people who have pretty much only witnessed the lack of that luster for the last two decades? I'll tell you how: **they never *decided* to believe—or Billieve, as it's said around here—in the Bills; the belief was passed down from the generation before them.**

When choosing a team to be your favorite, one usually chooses a team that is exciting to watch or fun to root for. The Bills have been neither of those things for a long time. But somehow, people my age keep showing love for this team that has mainly stunk up the joint in recent memory. But their parents, aunts, uncles, and other elders were in the prime of their lives when the Buffalo Bills were playing some of the best football in the country. It was fun. It was exciting. It was the best time to be a Bills fan. Then, when things got rough, those same people began to wax poetic about the glory days, telling their kids, nieces, and nephews about Jim Kelly, Thurman Thomas, Bruce Smith, and their sheer dominance. And so my peers looked to their elders with big, glowing eyes and decided that being a Bills fan was an amazing thing. There's no way it couldn't be given the stories they were hearing, right?

Wrong. Very, very wrong. Up until this past season, every Bills fan my age has suffered through mediocre year after mediocre year. They certainly didn't have to. There were other teams, other options of fanhood available to them. But they stuck to their guns and kept cheering under the guise of loyalty.

You may not be a Bills fan, but I'd be willing to bet that you have unconsciously chosen to suffer at some point in your life. The whole reason that my millennial peeps kept taking their lumps with the Bills was because they saw what their parents were doing and were like, "Alrighty, then. I love my parents, they seem like smart people, and they really love the Bills. I'm on board."

When you see older people who you love and trust acting a certain way or believing in particular things, you somewhat blindly sign off on those things for yourself. Why question what worked for them? After all, they seem like wise people. For many of my peers growing up, this meant becoming a devoted Bills fan. For you, this might mean thinking that money is the root of all evil, that marriage is a crock, or that gay people don't deserve love the same way straight people do. There is undoubtedly some thought, belief, or emotional state of being that you saw as a kid and bought into long before you were old enough to know what was good for you and what you truly believed. And as the wise Mahatma Ghandi once said:

"Your beliefs become your thoughts, Your thoughts become your words, Your words become your actions, Your actions become your habits, Your habits become your values, Your values become your destiny."

So, yeah. Some of these beliefs that you acquired at a young age have been causing you to speak a certain way and act a certain way, eventually creating habits that have embedded themselves into your subconscious mind. Your current autopilot setting was handed to you when you were a kid, and you didn't even know it.

> YOU MAY BE AN ADULT NOW, BUT
> IN SOME AREAS OF YOUR LIFE,
> 8-YEAR-OLD YOU IS DEFINITELY
> CALLING THE SHOTS.

Now, before you speed over to your parents' house and blame them for your shitty relationship or empty bank account, pump the brakes. You're an adult, and you are free to make your own choices. The fact that you haven't been aware of some of the reasons behind your choices until now isn't their (or anyone else's) fault. It's up to you to take responsibility and avoid playing the victim. More on that later.

To be honest, some of the thoughts and beliefs you downloaded from your environment—parents, teachers, commercials, etc.—could very well be gifts to you in the here and now. For instance, I grew up in a great family with amazing parents who clearly loved each other. My two siblings are awesome humans, and we all get along like old chums. This was the life that I grew up with.

So…guess what?

That is *exactly* what I wanted to recreate as I matured into adulthood. Give me a wife and some kids, wrap that up with a good portion of love, and I'd be all set. I yearned to repeat that cycle. But it wasn't because I went on a deep spiritual journey that led me to that place; I just witnessed a pretty awesome upbringing and figured that was how it went. I assumed that since I experienced a happy home, I would continue to be happy if I were to create one of my own. I'm ecstatic that this pattern of behavior and way of living was passed down to me. I'm glad I accepted it without much thought. What a gift.

But not everything that is passed down to us is for our greater good. Sometimes our parents and teachers as well as other influences from our environment send us mixed or even negative messages about self-worth, financial aptitude, (un)healthy relationships, and many other things. It's truly a mixed bag of attributes that we tend to accept as normal because of the love and trust that we have for the people who show us the way.

The Buffalo Bills aren't any good, but they have plenty of fans. Abusive relationships aren't healthy for anyone, but we all know someone who is involved in one. Overeating and under-exercising aren't smart plays, but there are a ton of people who buy into the lifestyle because it's what they saw when they were a kid. There are hundreds—if not thousands—of thoughts, beliefs, and little phrases floating around in your head that you never *truly* decided were yours. Hopefully this chapter will at least give you some awareness. This entire section of the book is written so that you can become more aware of the patterns that have been operating under the surface of your consciousness.

So, let's recap. You now know that change requires fighting what's familiar to you and that what's familiar to you (in the form of thoughts and beliefs) may very well be inherited from someone you loved and trusted as a kid. Now that you can see those two things for what they are, it should be easy to move past mediocre and chase your goals, right?

Sorry, friend.

Although we've lit up some dark corners of your subconscious mind, there's still some stuff that you need to see.

Chapter 4

That's How You Feel?

If you've bought this book and are reading these words, I'll take the liberty of assuming that one of the two following things is true for you:

1. You are a friend or a family member who bought my book to show your support and witness what I created. You're a special sort of human, and I have a ton of gratitude for your gesture of purchasing the book and actually reading this far.

2. You, like me, have read a fair number of personal development, self-help books and were looking for a fresh perspective to add to your collection.

No matter which category you fall into, let me take a minute to thank you for being here.

If you're riding with me in group two (or are a hybrid of the two categories), you've most definitely been exposed to the goal setting, #RiseAndGrind,

"Take Relentless Action" culture that is self-development. When I first started reading books that communicated that message, it lit a fire under my ass. It made me think about what I wanted, what I needed to do to make it happen, and how to go about doing it. It forced me to ask and answer questions that I'd always shrugged off before such as:

"Who am I?"

"What am I here for?"

"What do I want to create and leave behind before I die?"

It was a rabbit hole that I had been avoiding for most of my adult life, believing that daydreaming and thinking through how I'd respond to said questions were less important than doing the laundry or answering email. But now that I'm deep into that rabbit hole, I've realized that there's something missing from the message. You can create goals all you want, but until you figure out the *emotions* that you're really after, you're going to be sprinting toward a life of empty accomplishments.

You're always chasing a feeling. It's not the money, the house, the marriage, or the job. It's always, always, ALWAYS the feeling that is associated with the tangible stuff that your subconscious mind is locked in on. There's a reason for every goal you set, you just have to dig up some stuff in your subconscious mind to figure out what that is.

> IF WATCHING YOUR KID BE BORN
> OR FINALLY GETTING YOUR DREAM
> JOB LEFT YOU NUMB, YOU
> WOULDN'T BE HUMAN. THE
> "THING" IS NEVER THE THING. IT'S
> ALWAYS THE EMOTION IT
> GIVES YOU.

Let me rewind the clocks here to try and explain.

Back in the intro, I told you a little bit about a long-term relationship I had in my early twenties. I met this girl in college, and we dated all the way through graduation and beyond. All in all, we were together for about four and a half years. I was twenty years old when we began dating and twenty-four when I broke it off.

Now, let me tie a few concepts together that we've already talked about. In the last chapter, I spoke about my good fortune to see a loving marriage and happy family in the home that I grew up in. We were (and still are) a close-knit crew, and as I grew up I wanted to create a similar marriage and family life for myself. My unconscious goal was to get married and have some kids; you know, the whole happily ever after sort of thing.

My parents got married when they were twenty-one, and wouldn't you know it, I happened to be twenty-one in the midst of this relationship. I was in the prime of young adulthood, and it seemed as if the stars were aligning as my goal and the timeline that I believed to be appropriate came together.

But there was one minor problem: I wasn't feeling it.

Don't get me wrong, this girl was a good human being, never cheated on me (that I know of), and we didn't fight a ton. But the connection was dial-up, and what I wanted was broadband. I floated along in the relationship, watching time pass and resenting those months and years as I watched them slip away, unfulfilled.

In the back of my mind, I knew I wanted to be a married man and raise a family. I held onto that relationship because it seemed like a natural pathway to achieving everything I dreamed.

"We've been together for four and a half years, what's the sense in throwing that away when I could just as easily get married and have everything I ever wanted?"

My goal was marriage, and I could have had it if I wanted it. But it didn't feel right to me. I was missing a big piece of the puzzle, and my lack of awareness as to what that piece was trapped me in a world of unfulfilled days and weeks. I forgot about what my goal meant to me on an emotional level. I had lost touch with how I wanted to feel and kept hanging onto what I wanted to accomplish. What do most people want to feel when they dream about a marriage they can get on board with?

Love. Everyone wants love—whatever that means to you—in their marriage. I had focused so heavily on what I wanted to have **that I completely lost touch with how I wanted to *feel.*** I didn't feel the love, and yet I persisted. I wasn't happy, and yet I hung on. My emotions were what I was after all along, but I set them aside and gave all my focus to a tangible result like marriage and family. If I had married her, I would've been miserable. If I had had kids with her, I would've felt trapped.

Luckily, I didn't. My good friend, Jimmy, spoke words that I needed to hear that allowed me to grow a set big enough to end our relationship. I was going through the motions and, if I'm being honest, it wasn't fair to either of us. "You have to think about Number 1," he said. "You have to figure out what *you* want and make a decision that's best for you." And with that, I stepped out into the unknown as a single man, not knowing where I was headed, but certain it was better than where I was.

> NO GOAL WILL EVER BE GOOD
> ENOUGH IF YOU ONLY FOCUS ON
> THE TANGIBLE ITEM OR RESULT
> THAT YOU CAN HOLD IN YOUR
> HAND OR SEE WITH YOUR EYES.

The goal-setting process will undoubtedly start there, but you have to dig deeper. Underneath the surface is where you can really understand what you're after. Your subconscious mind holds a hidden treasure chest of secret motivations for the biggest dreams you have for your life. Those "secret" motivations are simply your emotions, but I'll bet that you don't spend too much time deeply thinking about how they play into your future and the ambitious aspirations you have.

YOU'RE SO EMOTIONAL

In our society, emotions are discussed in terms of how we react to things around us and what provokes us to feel a certain way.

Getting a raise at work will make you feel accomplished.

Taking a vacation will provoke the feeling of freedom.

Sharing a tight embrace with a family member will help you feel loved.

Getting dumped makes you feel lonely.

Walking down the street in the dark might make you feel fear.

This list could go on for a while, but you get the idea: **emotions tend to be viewed as reactionary responses to the stimuli around us.** Something happens and it makes you feel a certain way. That's how we identify with emotions. We think of them as an almost involuntary response to the world and the circumstances that surround us. In fact, if I mention someone and describe him as "emotional," what sort of person comes to mind? A calm, cool, and collected cat? Or someone who can't help but react to events in his life—whether those events are good or bad?

I'm going with the latter, and I'd bet that you chose similarly. It's because we equate emotional people to those who react to their environment the *strongest.* Of course we do. Our culture sees emotions through a lens of reaction, so it makes sense that someone classified as emotional seemingly can't control his reactions to the stimuli he comes across.

I have a tiny little secret though. It's one that your subconscious has been holding onto for a while, and it'll probably be pissed that I told you this. Your emotions play a much bigger role in your life than a simple knee-jerk reaction to a funny joke, scary scene, or sad story. Your emotions are the drivers of everything you do. They aren't simply reflective of how you react to the world around you. They are the reason you do anything worthwhile and pursue your wildest dreams. It's just that some of them are buried so deep below the surface of your ambitions that you don't ever recognize their presence or importance with your conscious mind.

We are all emotional, and until you actually embrace those emotions, you will always come up empty hearted when you get to where you thought you wanted to be. Let me try to paint the picture for you so you have a more concrete idea of how to avoid the empty, unfulfilled feeling of reaching your goal, only to find yourself disappointed.

BE PROACTIVE WITH YOUR EMOTIONS RATHER THAN REACTIVE

Take a deep breath, and as you exhale, let your biggest, most audacious goal float to the top of your mind. Is it an unforgettable vacation? Is it a dream job? Is it a picture perfect wedding day? Sit with whatever goal just popped into your head for a minute (take your time if need be, the words will still be here when you've found something that really gets you excited).

First, understand that what you're currently holding in your mind and heart is NOT the goal. That house, relationship, and rockin' bod are all just packaging. Inside the package and underneath the surface—the stomping grounds of the subconscious—you will find your real goal. Oh, what an interesting surprise...**it's a feeling you're after.**

You're chasing an emotion. That's it, that's all. You can now close the book and go about your day.

If only it were that easy.

Here's the hard part: the emotion that you desire is subconsciously attached to the tangible thing that you chase down every day. For instance, if your goal is to make $1,000,000 in the next year, you're probably really looking for an emotion like freedom, happiness, or worthiness. If your mind plays out the sentence, "Once I have the $1,000,000, I'll be [insert emotion here]," you're setting yourself up for a rough road.

Since you're wired to see emotions as a way to react to a circumstance, somewhere deep down you feel like you have to wait until the money's there to react with happiness, freedom, or worthiness. When you hit the finish line, you'll finally feel that it's appropriate to smile and embrace the emotion that you were after all along.

So, between Point A (where you currently are) and Point B (your million-dollar paycheck), guess what sort of feelings you'll be lacking along the way? Happiness, freedom, and worthiness. When you put off that feeling and wait for some moment in your make-believe future to express it, you're imprisoning yourself to NOT feel those amazing feelings until you've created a tangible reason to react that way.

That's a long journey of stress, hustle, and grind only to arrive at a small moment of satisfaction that you can't freeze in time. There's definitely a better way. **Rather than waiting to react with emotion, choose to be proactive in your conscious experience of those emotions.**

Let's use the desired $1,000,000 paycheck to hammer this point home. The three emotions that were probably attached to that goal were happiness, freedom, and worthiness. You might have other emotions in mind, and if so, roll with those. Instead of waiting for the finish line to let those emotions wash over you, choose to experience them every day. There is a way to feel happy, free, and worthy before you have $1,000,000 in the bank. If you want to feel happy, crank up your favorite tune and give your steering wheel the performance of a lifetime. If you want to feel free, go for a walk during your lunch hour instead of sitting at your desk and munching on that sandwich while scrolling through Facebook. If you want to feel worthy...well that's a gift given to you upon birth. You don't need a million bucks to be worthy of anything.

Having micro experiences of how you want to feel—with my clients I call this "taking hits of emotion"—will do two things for you:

Keep you Focused on What You Want

What you focus on and give your energy to expands. If you are consistently bringing some happiness or freedom into your world, you will find that there is more happiness and freedom to appreciate. *Sidenote: For my people in the back with the "Yeah, I wish" expression tattooed on their face, you're living proof of this fact. A cynical, pessimistic perspective will only bring you more things to question and be sarcastic about. So pivot that perspective and focus toward what you want rather than the sourpuss you're rocking.*

Make You Less Needy

Have you ever witnessed (or been a part of) a relationship where one partner was the neediest human alive? Where they needed their partner to validate their existence, make them feel good all the time, and never leave them feeling lonely? It's cringeworthy, really. In almost all cases, what does the needy party do to their partner? Repel them! You may be just as needy about reaching your goal. You may look at your aspirations and your progress toward them as something needed to validate you, make you feel good, and never leave your side. That's Repelling 101. By getting small doses of those emotions ahead of time, though, you won't *need* the finish line so badly that you keep pushing it further away. Small hits of emotions daily will allow you to enjoy the process without being so desperate about the outcome.

Your feelings are more powerful than you've probably ever considered, and by harnessing their power daily, you can unearth them from your subconscious mind. Up until now, they've just been lying dormant under the surface, popping up every now and then like a game of emotional whack-a-mole. Instead of waiting to feel a certain emotion or being surprised when it shows up uninvited, lean into your feelings every single day. Not only that, choose the ones that you desire to feel in some far-off future, and then find ways to bring them into the next twenty-four hours of your existence.

THE MORE NATURALLY YOU CAN GENERATE THE EMOTIONS YOU DESIRE FOR YOUR FUTURE, THE MORE LIKELY THAT FUTURE BECOMES. IF YOU'RE USED TO THE EXPERIENCE OF AN EMOTION, IT MAKES IT EASY TO CREATE MORE MOMENTS THAT INSPIRE IT.

Own the art of being emotional and know that you get to choose how you feel. Set your emotional tone each day rather than sliding back into the habit of re-acting unconsciously. By pointing your emotional compass toward something you want to feel, you will begin to move past all the feelings you'd rather not mess with. You're not a victim to your circumstances or your subconscious mind's interpretation of them.

Chapter 5

Success is Subconsciously Scary

No one is immune to fear. Everywhere you go to- day you will pass someone who is scared of losing their job, scared that their parent is dying, or scared that they might be heading toward divorce. Show me someone who says they're not scared of anything, and I'll show you a liar.

But the context of fear that we humans tend to ob- serve most often is that of failure, disappointment, or tragedy. We fear the negative. We fear the "no" that comes in response to our hopeful questions. We fear rejection. You're probably nodding your head in agreement because these forms of fear are all very familiar to us. It doesn't seem abnormal to be afraid of life dealing us a shitty hand. Fear is two-faced, however. Failure is NOT the only thing that makes you shake in your metaphorical boots.

You are just as scared of success.

You may be tempted to call bullshit here, but stay with me. You fear failure and tragedy because they disrupt the status quo of your life. If you have a job, then all of a sudden lose that job, it rocks your proverbial boat. If you propose to your girlfriend with the expectation that she'll say yes and she doesn't, that's a sucker punch to your emotional gut. It's scary because if what you fear were to actually happen, it would change your life and rob you of the zone of familiarity you have grown accustomed to.

Guess what? Success changes your life, too. The change may come in the sense that you're objectively moving in a more positive direction, but it's change all the same. And your subconscious mind is NOT a huge fan of change.

FEAR OF YES

Fear of failure is old hat. Anybody with a pulse is scared of rejection, messing up, or looking dumb in front of people they care about. If I went out and asked 100 random people on the street if they hated the idea of failing, all of them (who are honest with themselves, anyway) would confirm this notion.

Fear of failure is the fear of No. The thought of getting a negative response to the question, "Am I [good, smart, attractive, experienced] enough to succeed?" scares the hell out of you. You're not alone, don't worry.

The opposite, however, can be just as scary.

> SINCE FAILURE THREATENS THE NORMS OF YOUR LIFE, IT'S SCARY. EVEN THOUGH SUCCESS IS "GOOD" CHANGE, IT IS CHANGE NONETHELESS. YOUR SUBCONSCIOUS MIND HATES CHANGE,

The fear of success—the kind of fear that not many of us want to own up to—is the fear of Yes. It is the fear that someone or something might *actually* yield to your desires and agree to your terms. But what's so frightening about getting everything you want? Why would that be scary? Because when you get someone to go out with you, pay you for your expertise, or give you that promotion you've been busting your ass for, **you have to make good on the value that you advertised.** You have to show up and deliver. You have to rise to the occasion.

It plays out like this: you ask that beautiful woman out—you know, the one you didn't think you had a shot with—and she says yes.

"Oh shit. Now I have to get her to like me!"

You declare the price of your product or service—you know, the price that you're uncomfortable to say out loud—and they agree to pay up.

"Oh god, now I have to show that I'm worthy of that cash."

You ask your boss for a long overdue promotion—after sweating it out for the last six months—and they agree to it with little resistance.

"Oh boy, I'm not sure I'm really ready for that responsibility."

When you're afraid of someone saying yes to your powerful requests, you are fearful of your own success, plain and simple.

Again, a little louder for the people in the back, anything that threatens what is familiar to you will inherently make you unsettled and uncomfortable. The potential of falling below the status quo makes you feel like a failure, while the potential of rising above what you're used to gets you all sweaty and nervous. In either case, subconscious fear takes the wheel and swerves you into a ditch.

The erratic behavior that your fear of failure is responsible for makes sense. But why would your subconscious sabotage your shot at success?

ARE YOU WORTHY?

There's a statistic that I've read in books and heard on podcasts that I always figured was a bit exaggerated. It was about people who had won the lottery or had a ton of money fall into their laps, only to squander every last penny. You would think that a lottery winner who previously lived paycheck to paycheck might do everything they could to hang onto their newfound riches. From what I've heard, though, that's not the case. I turned to Google to see how accurate the numbers were because, like I said, the percentage of people who were said to have lost it all felt way too big to be real.

After doing some diligent research (reading the first three articles Google delivered to me), it seemed as though the numbers in fact don't lie. Roughly seventy percent of lottery winners burn their financial houses to the ground and file for bankruptcy. In fact, lottery winners are twice as likely to file for bankruptcy than the average human being. Winning the lottery is a windfall of financial success, but the majority of the people who are lucky enough to experience it flush it down the toilet. If, on the day their lucky number was drawn, you asked them if they were scared of the fat check they were about to receive, do you think they would own up to being afraid of their winnings? That's a hard no. Not much to be (consciously) scared of when your bank account suddenly has more digits than your phone number. And yet, when they enter a level of financial success that they hadn't dreamt possible, they shoot themselves in the foot with a self-sabotaging shotgun.

The lottery winners who lose it all don't have exclusive rights to the concept of squandering their own success, though. You've likely experienced the sour taste of a crushing defeat following one of your own greatest victories as well.

You see, we've all spent years programming our thoughts, actions, and beliefs through a series of mostly unconscious habits. We wake up and live our own version of Groundhog Day ninety percent of the time, leaving little room for nuance and new experiences. Because of this, our mind and body get plenty of repetitions within the identity that we believe ourselves to be. After a while, we tend to slide into a sense of normalcy.

You used to call this your comfort zone, but you now know that it's really just a zone of familiarity.

Anyway, within this zone of familiarity, you become accustomed to a certain level of worthiness. Whether you chose to decide your worth for yourself or allowed someone else to give you their stamp of approval, you've settled on a certain level of worthiness that you're cool with. Think of it as a Worthiness Thermostat. You'd prefer that it stay right where you have it because you're used to it and have come to accept it.

If you or someone around you attempts to lower your level of worthiness, you will likely rally to bring your levels back up. You like that unworthy feeling about as much as you enjoy it being fifty-six degrees in your living room in the middle of winter. With that in mind, you crank things up to do what you can to return to homeostasis. That, after all, is the purpose of a thermostat: to regulate the temperature back to one you're comfortable with.

Experiencing success (or potential success) challenges the opposite end of your Worthiness Thermostat. It raises your levels high enough that your subconscious mind kicks on to start bringing you back down to earth. You know how the AC kicks on when it gets too hot in order to cool things back down? Your subconscious Worthiness Thermostat will do the same if you begin to entertain the idea of operating out of your league.

Let's bring those lottery winners back into the picture. Before they hit it big, their level of financial worthiness was likely at a much lower level. On one hand, they were ecstatic about coming into millions of dollars. On the other hand, the fact that they didn't have to work for their new abundance of cash runs in direct contrast to what they have grown accustomed to. They went from working hard just to get by to never having to work for anything. Just when they thought life couldn't get better, their Worthiness Thermostat kicked on.

Thoughts like, "You don't deserve this money" and "You need to help [insert emotional personal connection] with all of this money," creep in and give them reason after reason to squander it all. Even though they'd love to keep the status of millionaire, their subconscious mind and its Worthiness Thermostat are fighting like hell to get them back to a state of what they consider to be normalcy.

Obviously, I'm not here to talk your ear off about millionaires who've gone broke. You have a Worthiness Thermostat, too. There is a certain level of success that your subconscious mind is willing to tolerate. Deep down under the surface of your brain, you believe you aren't worthy of much more than what you currently have. If you start acting too big for your britches, you may find yourself burning your ambitions to the ground. It's just your subconscious mind trying to regulate the system.

JUST LIKE THE THERMOSTAT
HANGING ON THE WALL AT YOUR
HOUSE, YOU HAVE THE POWER TO
GET UP AND CHANGE WHAT LEVEL
OF SUCCESS, HAPPINESS, AND
LOVE YOU TOLERATE VIA YOUR
WORTHINESS THERMOSTAT.

EXPERT TIP: AIM HIGH

To the outside world, you might say something like, "I'm really going to do it this time! I'm going to crush these goals!" At which point your subconscious mind will just sit back and whisper, "It's adorable that you think you can have more than what you currently have. We're safe here. We're comfy here. We know what to expect here. We're not going anywhere." The more you become aware of its trickery, however, the more you can sidestep your subconscious' attempt at keeping you stuck when you're ready to grow. The resistance that sneaks in when you're about to take a leap of faith toward your dreams is just a last-ditch effort from the depths of your mind to preserve your safety.

Your subconscious mind isn't evil, it just doesn't want to see you get hurt. It believes safety is found within the boundaries of what you're used to. But you can grow, expand, and change and still be safe. Success should bring celebration, not a shiver down your spine. Let this chapter give you enough awareness to begin seeing that you can have more and are worthy of more if you so choose it. There's nothing to be scared of, my friend. Step boldly toward that which inspires you.

Chapter 6

Training Day

My wife and I have a little pup named Maggie. She's not really a pup anymore, being eight years old, but she'll always be our puppy despite any gray hairs that may sprout. She's a little twenty-pound Cavalier King Charles Spaniel. I know the breed sounds pretentious, but she really is a sweet little dog. She cuddles, gives hugs, and even sings (squeals) with joy when my wife or I give her some good rubs.

One thing she doesn't do so well? Listen. If you were to Google something along the lines of "Benefits of Owning a Cavalier King Charles Spaniel," almost every link on the first page would contain information about how easy they are to train, how obedient they can be, and how loyally they listen to their owners.

Maggie must not have been included in this study.

She's not a terror to us or our home by any means, but we've got her trained about as well as our six-month-old daughter, Lucy. You ask her to come, she stays. You ask her to stay, she comes. And don't even get me started on her fetching skills. Fetch, the calling card of all dogs, has been Maggie's greatest struggle of all. She'll get all excited at the sight of a ball ready for launch, chase it down as it's being thrown, then stand over the ball and just bark. She doesn't pick it up. She doesn't bring it back. She just barks as if the audible sound she makes will solve the problem.

She's our fur baby, and we love her, but she doesn't do so well with following directions. Our training efforts have been subpar, and I read on the internet somewhere that you can't teach an old dog new tricks. Luckily, she's cute, so the incessant barking during what might be perceived as a game of fetch isn't the worst thing in the world. Your subconscious mind is a lot like Maggie. If you haven't done a good job of training it, there's a good chance it's going to do a lot of stuff that you'd prefer it didn't.

You'll tell yourself that you want to lose a handful of pounds, then find yourself walking straight to the freezer for a pint of ice cream for no good reason.

You'll tell yourself that you're ready to date again, then that subconscious of yours will get you to scroll through Instagram for hours instead of hopping on match.com and committing to the process.

You'll tell yourself that you're going to buckle down and start a business that you're passionate about, and your cute little subconscious will highlight all the ways that you don't have the time or money to do that right now.

> WHEN YOU SET OUT TO DO SOMETHING OUTSIDE OF YOUR FAMILIAR ZONE, JUST PICTURE YOUR SUBCONSCIOUS MIND SAYING "BLESS YOUR HEART" IN A SARCASTIC SOUTHERN ACCENT.

In the same way Maggie stays put when I tell her to come, there's a good chance that your untrained subconscious mind isn't following your directions very well. Thankfully, there's a good reason for this. All of your hopes and dreams are conscious thoughts, while your actions and behaviors are most likely patterns that have lived under the surface for a while. What you say you want and what you habitually do don't live on the same plane.

But there's hope! You can teach an old dog new tricks. That is, you can train your subconscious mind, even if it's been running around without a leash for decades. Wouldn't it be nice to actually make your conscious wishes come true?

COMMUNICATING YOUR CONSCIOUSNESS

Now that you've learned a lot about your subconscious and its powers, I hope that it brings you comfort to know that you can train it; you just need to be a better communicator.

When you have big ideas and grand goals, they begin above the surface, up in your conscious mind. But as you've noticed, it's your subconscious mind that's sort of driving the bus. On top of that, your subconscious mind is the land of habits and patterns of behavior that have been practiced repeatedly. Whether it be the skill of driving or the belief that money doesn't grow on trees, any thought that's gotten plenty of conscious reps in your life will eventually become an automatic program in your subconscious.

Therefore, in order for a fleeting thought of your amazing future to take hold and be acted upon by your subconscious mind, it needs to be practiced and repeated so that it can become second nature. If you're only mulling over what you want to manifest every so often, you'll find that your accomplishments are about as inconsistent as your attempts to visualize them. Your conscious mental reps are just as important as your physical reps at the gym. If you only do a couple, you probably won't see much of a difference. If you really commit to the process and do the reps required to grow, you will download your desires to your subconscious mind over time. Here's one of the best ways you can start reppin' today:

AFFIRM THAT SHIZZ

My introduction to affirmations wouldn't fall into the category of "traditional." It wasn't some guru who turned me on to them or some podcast that extolled their many benefits.

It was Michael Jordan.

I remember watching Mike and resident life coach of the Saturday Night Live set, Stuart Smalley, look into a mirror and repeat positive affirmations to themselves, the most memorable being, "I'm good enough, I'm smart enough, and doggone it...people like me!" Of course, SNL put on this display in jest, but as I've researched and implemented this stuff over the last few years, I've come to realize the amazing value of affirmations.

By repeating positive affirmations to yourself, you can begin to slowly shift the landscape of your subconscious mind. Affirmations like, "I am abundant" or "I am loved" may seem like silly little sentences, but the more you hear yourself say them, the more you begin to believe it. You may have to choke down some sarcasm in the beginning, but you'll find that you'll believe your words more and more as time passes. Maybe the resistance lessens, maybe it's an acquired taste; either way, it goes down smoother the more often you do it.

Another great aspect about affirming your power through these simple phrases is that they are short and easy to remember. You're not reprogramming your subconscious mind via a dissertation-length mantra. You're creating bite-sized phrases to remember and log in to your bank of thoughts for easy access. Because of this, you won't have to think about these affirmations after a while. Instead, you'll have quick and easy access to them due to their simplicity.

One small, subtle nuance of affirmations that's worth mentioning here is that they **need to be said and presented in the present tense.** Don't tiptoe into the land of, "I will be [insert trait or characteristic] someday."

When you say to yourself that you will be something, you're openly acknowledging that you aren't yet that thing. If you keep doubling down on a statement like, "I will be rich someday" or "I will lose twenty pounds," you are stacking up more and more opportunities to shine a bright light on what you lack.

> THERE AREN'T MANY THINGS
> MORE DISEMPOWERING THAN
> REPEATEDLY SHOWING LOVE TO
> THE GAP BETWEEN YOU AND
> YOUR GOALS.

So, keep your affirmations present tense, and own whatever you are stepping into with each statement. Sometimes, what you say won't even be true in your objective reality, but in order for it to become more than just a possibility, you need to get your subconscious mind and its powerful, habit-driven behavior on board. Get that megaphone out and start yelling about all the things that you are.

FEEL YOUR WAY INTO IT

One last thing before we tie a bow on this chapter. Delivering repetitive thoughts and words to your subconscious is a necessity if you want to change your world. You gotta feed the beast. But if you're doing it half-assed, the practice will be in vain. It would be the equivalent of going to the gym and standing at the squat rack scrolling through Instagram. In each case, even though you've put yourself in the position to strengthen yourself, you aren't really getting much done. And if you're the guy just standing at the squat rack, you're kind of an asshole.

In order to get the full effect of affirmations and any other communication that you serve up to your subconscious mind, you need to feel aligned with what you're saying.

Raise your hand if this (or something similar) has happened to you. You woke up and felt ready to take on the world. As you sipped your morning coffee with a smile, you said to yourself, "I'm going to start my own business" or "I'm going to quit my job and travel the world" or "I'm finally going to get back in the gym and get myself back in shape." You know, one of those monologues that is going to change everything. And then, just as soon as you put your dreams into words, you heard the soft whisper of your inner critic in your ear, reminding you of all the reasons that you most definitely would not do all of the things that you just said you'd do. Even though your words were po-etic and intentional, that little inner critic mustered up a feeling that was in direct conflict with your goals.

If I had to sum up what keeps so many people stuck, it is THAT moment right there. The moment when thoughts and words about one's potential in life are incongruent with their emotions and beliefs about what is possible.

You can say, "I am abundant" all you want, but if you serve it up with a subconscious side of, "Well, that's bullshit," you don't have a chance. Affirmations are as useful as the emotions that they're backed by. Now for the fun part: **emotions can be manufactured.** If you're looking for some genuine happiness to pair with an affirmation like "I am content," you can bring that emotion to life on the spot. Just as we talked about earlier in the book, emotions aren't just alarms that go off when something is happening around us; they can be brought to life within us on command. With that in mind, you've got to conjure up the emotion required to align your subconscious with whatever positive affirmation you're declaring.

"But Nick, how am I supposed to feel aligned with happiness, abundance, or peace when I don't have any of that in my life right now?"

Don't be so emotionally lazy, that's how. Physical evidence isn't required in order to feel anything. You don't need the overflowing bank account to feel abundant, a perfect marriage to feel love, or a vacation to Bali in order to feel free. All of those things make it easier to feel those emotions, but it's not the only way to access them. If you think you have to have "that thing" in order to feel something, you are being emotionally lazy.

I have a feeling that perhaps you're not quite on board. Let's try this on for size. Think about a movie or TV show that sucker punched you right in your feelings. It snuck up from behind and smothered you with emotion at a moment when you weren't prepared to ugly cry in front of your family. Just throw on any episode of *This Is Us* if you're having trouble coming up with an example. The point is, the real emotions that you felt in your body were a result of a fictional character doing some stuff in a make-believe world. Real emotions. Fake world. If Jack Pearson can get your emotional juices flowing from the other side of your TV screen, you better believe you can create some stories that are just as moving. There are two main ways to cook those feelings up in your emotional crockpot (too soon?):

Experience

Even though you may not have clear evidence of a certain emotion in your life right now, odds are pretty good that you've experienced the emotion you're after at some point. For instance, if you're lacking confidence, you may want to implement affirmations to deliver confidence to your subconscious mind...but you don't feel as though you have any confidence to lean on and believe in. If you dig into the treasure trove of memories you have stored away, there will undoubtedly be something in there that will remind you what confidence feels like. Maybe it was a heroic moment in a little league baseball game or the image of yourself walking across stage at college graduation. You most likely have something you can pull on or tap into. Sit with that moment for a few minutes. Think about the details, the beautiful parts about it that made it special to you. And then, once you've let the memory simmer for a bit...guess what? Confidence will be running through your veins here in 2019 (or whatever year you're reading this) even though your memory is from 1995. Use that emotion now to powerfully affirm your confidence to your subconscious mind.

Imagination

Neville Goddard once said, "This world is brought into being by man's imagination." When we're little, we use imagination all the time. When we get older, that same imagination gets swapped for a paycheck, some bills, and a strong dose of reality. But just as every fictional character was birthed from imagination, we can also create stories and scenes for ourselves that will evoke the emotions we seek to align with. You can imagine what abundance, love, and happiness all feel like. It's just a matter of being creative enough to dream it, then willing to sit with it until it feels real enough to spark an emotion.

By digging into your past experiences or using a little imagination, you can come face to face with the emotions that will supercharge your affirmations. When you couple powerful affirmations with meaningful emotions, your subconscious will have to give in over time.

Remember how we talked about the fact that it's not strange to drive all the way home without even thinking about how you got there? Wouldn't it be cool if it were equally not bizarre when thoughts like "I am strong" or "Money flows to me easily" were as automatic as your driving skills?

Teach your old dog new tricks. Start training your mind today.

Chapter 7

Storytime with Your Subconscious Mind

What is life without meaning? Sorry to slap you with a deep existential question right off the bat, but walk with me for a minute.

Sometimes, the meaning that we attach to events and circumstances can make our lives miserable. Think back to your greatest heartbreak. That heart wrenching, soul-numbing experience wasn't the most fun you've ever had. But it's not because of the other person's actions. It was because of the meaning that *you* cooked up as a result. They decided that they weren't interested in dating you anymore, and your mind did something like this:

"Well, if they don't want to date me, then I guess I'm not that attractive. I guess I'm not as funny as I thought I was. I guess I didn't make her happy. May-

be I'm not capable of doing that for someone else. Maybe I'm selfish. Maybe I'll never find someone else to put up with me. Maybe I'm not worthy of love..."

The rabbit hole can get pretty deep, but I'll stop there. You don't need to see every last detail of the downward spiral to know that it's real. You've experienced a similar slide when you've been rejected or dismissed. But it was all your mind's fault. It loves to create storylines and place meaning on everything that occurs in your life. There's a reason that movies and cinema will always be held near and dear to the human heart: we love narrative and compelling storytelling because we do it to ourselves all day long.

One person rejects you and all of a sudden you create a story that lands you at, "I'm not lovable."

Jesus.

This meaning-making machine that sits between our ears seems pretty toxic, right? Maybe we should just try to scrap our ability to create those stories. It seems like we'd be better off if we could just be super objective and see things for what they are rather than seeing everything through the lens of what it means to each of us. But, I'm afraid that would make life about as boring as your high school biology textbook. Living a life without meaning would leave you with little more than facts, figures, and data.

Besides, our ability to create storylines and narratives isn't *all* bad. You know all those fond memories you have of early Christmas mornings, sun-filled vacations, and late nights in college? Those are all stories that you've created as well. You might think that since you experienced the event, your mind has simply stored a nonfiction retelling of the moments that transpired. But you'd be wrong. Your memories are about as factual as the movie *Titanic*. Sure, a big boat sank in the ocean, but the details of Rose and Jack's love affair were scripted to give meaning and a storyline to the overarching setting of the story.

When you wax poetic about your childhood or all the awesome things you did in your early twenties, you're likely painting a picture that's slightly fictional as well. When moments become sentimental, your mind will literally filter out the bad and reimagine the good with brighter colors, bigger smiles, and louder laughter. These memories mean so much to you, so you tend to throw an Instagram filter on what really went down to preserve those precious moments.

You remember your sixteenth birthday party with reverence because your parents surprised you with a car, all your best friends were in attendance, and you all danced the night away without a care in the world. Everyone had an amazing time and still talk about it to this day. But what your mind *forgot* to mention is that your brother's ex-girlfriend showed up to the party drunk, had to be asked to leave, and didn't go quietly. In comparison to all of the other objectively awesome things that happened that night, your mind kind of ignores that part of the evening. The meaning that you have attached to that memory is one of love, excitement, and fun, so the drunk ex-girlfriend gets cut from the script as time goes on.

Or, maybe you recall how thrilling it was to win the championship game back when you played baseball in high school. You were awarded MVP after hitting a home run and making some great plays at third base. They carried you off the field and chanted your name as you left. But what you tend to block out of that amazing memory is what drove you to such a performance. Your parents told you just twenty-four hours earlier that they were getting a divorce. You showed up to the game needing an outlet to release your frustration, and the baseball you hit 450 feet was happy to help you out. But yeah, your mind doesn't give much love to that family meeting that crushed you. It just remembers the exhilaration of hearing your own name bellow through the stadium. Once again, the memory of coming out as champs trumps the relative facts of that day, so you look back and omit certain details to make those moments glow a little brighter in your mind.

So, the ability to create meaning and storylines in your mind is both good and bad. Sometimes, it runs you off the road into a ditch of negative self-talk when you get rejected. Sometimes, it makes your memories seem like a movie that you can't get enough of. Whether it's good or bad, the meaning-making machine that is your mind will keep showing up and doing its thing.

It's just a matter of which direction you *choose* to let it go.

CHOOSE A STORY THAT SERVES YOU

Throughout your entire life, your mind (mostly the subconscious side, surprise surprise) has been writing narrative after narrative to give meaning to the world around you and the events within that world. There's even a story that's being written in your mind right now entitled *What It Means to Read Nick's Book*. I hope it's a good one.

If you're reading this book to gain some inspiration to better your life, the story that your mind is creating is centered around how you're making a positive choice for yourself. Go you! If you're a friend or a family member who picked this up to support my mission, your story may be more of a mental pat on the back, acknowledging that you are showing love to this thing that I put a lot of energy into. It doesn't matter what your particular narrative looks like, I'm simply here to make you aware that there *is* one.

So many of us wander aimlessly through life, assuming that the stories that we hear in our heads are universal to everyone else's experience. They're not.

YOU MAY THINK YOU SEE THE
WORLD AS IT IS, BUT YOU'RE
REALLY VIEWING IT THROUGH
YOUR VERY OWN, VERY SKEWED
PRESCRIPTION LENSES.

Jay-Z is closing in on being worth a billion dollars—that's with a *B*. As of this writing, he's sold thirty-six million albums. But countless men and women who were also raised in the Marcy Projects with Sean Carter can't even sniff that level of success. Why? Because Jay-Z saw what he didn't like about his upbringing, then worked his ass off to never live like that again. Everyone else told a story that kept them stuck in the projects. His story, however, was an empowering one. It made him the hero who would eventually escape his circumstances and become one of the greatest rappers and businessmen of all time.

What if your parents got divorced? Some see that as a reason to never choose love because they've witnessed its destruction. Others will hold love in such a bright light that no Negative Nancy or Neal could ever shake them of what they want. Those who veer away from love have created a story around why it sucks. On the other hand, those who seek love and marriage created a story similar to Jay-Z's; they witnessed the worst and now know that they want the opposite.

The story that you tell yourself about yourself is important. The meaning that you give to the things that have happened to you will ultimately determine your perspective and the point of view from which you see the world as well as your place in it. It's your job to choose a story that serves you in the highest way possible.

The hardest part about choosing the right story is having the awareness that you have the option to do so. Again, up until this point, your subconscious mind has had a tight grip on the reins as you've ridden through life. It's been making decisions, embedding beliefs, and performing actions without your consent ever since you were a little boy or girl. You shouldn't be surprised, then, that it has had a permanent seat at the head of the table in the writer's room of your mind. It's time for a good old-fashioned coup d'état.

THE RIGHT STORY NEEDS THE RIGHT LENS

In order to choose the right narrative for your life, you need to start seeing it through the right lens.

I've been wearing glasses since the fifth grade. When I first got them, I remember being mortified to the point that I wouldn't wear them at school. I didn't want to be labeled The Nerd at such an early age, I guess. I'd leave the house with them on, but once I got on the bus, I tucked them in my bookbag. Kids will be kids.

Anyway, guess what? Without my glasses, I couldn't see a damn thing. I squinted and acted like it was all good, but in reality, it would have been a lot easier if I'd only realized that the lenses were there to help me, not put me in a corner of angsty nerdiness. I quite literally wasn't seeing my world through the right lens, and it made my life harder than it had to be.

When it comes to the stories that are stored in your brain, you likely could use a fresh perspective on some of their plot lines. It might be good for you to try on some new lenses and see if things can be seen a little more clearly or, at the very least, are a little more pleasant to look at.

Tony Robbins is famous for saying, "Life isn't happening to you, it's happening *for* you." Tony's not an optometrist or anything, but this is a pretty powerful prescriptive lens through which to look back and view your life. With this lens, you can begin to find positive meaning in many of the events that you may have deemed the darkest moments of your life.

Take a second and think back on some of the moments in your life that you'd rather forget. Do some inventory on what you can remember, and do your best to pull the facts from your fictional retelling of the events that occurred. Like I said before, your subconscious mind has probably painted a pretty ugly picture of the memories of your biggest heartbreak or the death of a family member. That meaning-making machine of yours can dream up some real horror stories if it feels like it.

With as many facts in hand as you can muster and the words of Mr. Robbins to lean on, ask yourself the following very powerful questions:

How was that [insert heart wrenching, soul sucking moment] good for me?

What did I learn about myself after going through that?

How did it benefit my life's path?

The first few answers that come to mind may be laced with cuss words aimed in my direction, but once you get that out of your system, really try to find legitimate responses to these questions. It's with honest responses to the questions above that you can begin to create a fresher and more helpful lens to see those past traumas through.

If your parents got divorced when you were young, dig deep and lean in to why it may have been beneficial to you. Your entire love life and your view of relationships up until this point may have been shaped by the story your subconscious created about your parents splitting. By consciously focusing on the good that came from that situation, you can begin to change the narrative around what love means to you.

Maybe their struggles as a couple showed you exactly what you didn't want for yourself when you grew up. Knowing what you don't want is just as valuable as knowing what you do want. Maybe watching your mom become a strong, independent woman in the process empowered you as a little girl. At the very least, you can look back and know that, even if your parents were a toxic match, they still produced you. I mean, that's a win, right? Trying on these new lenses as you look back at your perceived facts of your past will allow you to rewrite that story in a powerful way.

If you lost a loved one to disease, maybe it reminded you of your mortality and lit a fire in you to live life to the fullest.

If you were cheated on, remind yourself that they did you favor. You wouldn't want to live a life with someone who clearly doesn't value you as much as they said they did.

If you lost your job, reframe that crushing blow as a new opportunity to explore your interests and discover what you're really meant to do. You hated that job anyway, remember? Getting the axe was a gift in disguise.

Find the beauty within the suck. Dig deep for gratitude within the stories that you have spent a lot of time trying to avoid. There is a gift in everything that happens for us in life. It's either moving us toward our best life or showing us exactly what not to do along the way. Put a new lens on that old story and appreciate the good that came from it.

> THE ONLY STORY THAT MATTERS IS THE ONE THAT YOU PUT YOUR HEART AND SOUL BEHIND. EVERYONE ELSE'S "FACTS" OF THE MATTER ARE IRRELEVANT. SEE AND BELIEVE IN **YOUR** TRUTH.

Your subconscious mind may freak out for a minute when you try to go back to those old stories, as its main mission is to keep you safe. But as you do revisit those old narratives, remind yourself that putting a new lens on and creating a new story will ultimately be more safe and secure for your soul than holding onto the hate, jealousy, frustration, or guilt that you used to pair with those dark moments. Press on and be the storyteller who lifts up your inner being.

Chapter 8

You Can Have It All

I never really watched the show *Friends* growing up. I'd catch an episode here or there when it was in syndication, but it was usually on in the background while I was grading papers or folding laundry.

My wife, however, is a huge fan of the show. I'm talking pre-Netflix. When the show made its way onto the streaming service that keeps most of us planted on the couch for more than an hour at a time *Friends* was introduced to many people who never got around to watching it when it was on the air. Not my wife, no no. She had the box set of all ten seasons on DVD well before you could stream the show at the click of a button.

When we first started hanging out, she asked if I was into the six buddies from NYC and their decade's worth of television. When I told her that I never really got into it, she looked at me with an expression that translated to "Settle in buddy, because we've got eighty-five hours of the best TV you've ever seen to watch."

At first I watched because I liked my then-girlfriend and wanted to make her happy. Cuddling up to her on the couch for an extended period of time was an added bonus. But I gotta say, over time, I genuinely started to enjoy the show. One character who was hard to dislike was the lovable buffoon, Joey Tribbiani. Joey was equal parts womanizer and lover of food but pulled it off with his comically low IQ and well-timed charm. He loved himself a good meatball sandwich but had a sweet tooth for the many ladies in his life as well. One scene in particular put his two largest loves in competition with one another.

Everyone was sitting around the coffee table at their favorite spot, Central Perk, watching Monica have a little too much fun while eating a piece of cake. After watching her seductively take each bite, Phoebe asked, if she had to give up food or sex, which one she would pick. Without thinking, Monica blurts out, "Sex!" with her poor husband, Chandler, sitting right next to her. Ouch.

The question that was posed was intriguing enough that they decided to go around the table and share which one they would part ways with if they had to choose. When the discussion made its way over to Joey, he had a really hard time picking one over the other. At first, he said he'd ditch food, then changed his mind and decided that maybe he'd get rid of sex. That didn't stick for long as he pivoted back to his original position of parting ways with food. This back and forth carried on for a few moments until he said, "I want both! I want girls on bread!"

I love this scene because Joey was given two choices: a) give up food or b) give up sex. He said to hell with all of that and chose to have both. He decided that he doesn't have to choose between the two things he loves and that he gets to have it all, in the form of girls on bread.

If we could all be as brave as Joey Tribbiani.

Every day that we walk this earth, we are faced with choices. We are given a buffet of options, plenty of things that we can commit our time and energy to. We play an infinite game of "this or that," choosing to say yes to some task or activity while simultaneously saying no to a host of others. But when we come to a decision whereby we have to choose between two things we love, we believe we can only have one of them. And, like Joey, we have a really hard time choosing. We feel conflicted and frustrated that we only get to have one and not the other.

I remember having a hard time with this inner conflict when I was getting my life coaching business off the ground. At the time, I had just become a dad, and there was nothing I wanted more than to be a great family man for my wife and new daughter. But, I also really wanted to create a successful coaching practice that would give us a little more financial freedom while allowing me to impact my clients in a big way. Also in the mix was my attempt to balance those responsibilities with being a full-time high school teacher.

I was trying to make it all work and flow naturally, but I often found myself overwhelmed, thinking that something had to fall by the wayside. My conscious mind was all like, "You got this, let's go out there and be somebody!" My subconscious mind countered with, "You're going to have to cut something out of the agenda here. You can't have too much going on at once."

There was an internal war that waged in the depths of my mind, and for a while it resulted in neither side winning. I didn't give up on my ambitions of being an amazing dad and husband, and I didn't let my life coaching dream die, either. I put a lot of energy into both (admittedly more into being a family man, more on that later) but didn't see much progress.

Why? Because as much as I wanted to have my cake and eat it, too, my subconscious mind held the ultimate trump card. It held the belief that I had to pick one thing and get rid of the other. As much as I knew I desired everything, my subconscious mind wasn't going to let me have it until I either a) parted ways with one of my goals or b) really wrestled with the idea that I had to choose one or the other.

I chose the second option. Rather than letting my subconscious mind win, I decided to dig into that belief and see if it was true or not. Going to battle with your subconscious mind isn't the easiest thing in the world, but luckily, I had my own coach to support me in my mission. He asked some questions that allowed me to see what was getting in my way.

Even though I talked a big talk and said I wanted to have it all, under the surface I didn't think it was possible. And if it were, in fact, possible, I was terrified of what might happen. I was scared that if my business took off, I would have less time with my family. I was scared that if I devoted all of my time to my wife and daughter, I would lose a sense of myself and my purpose in life. I was scared to have it all. I felt like choosing one would be the safer and less stressful option. And since our subconscious mind prefers safety to the unknown, I kept finding myself accomplishing little more than spinning my wheels.

In just one conversation, my coach, Preston, helped me see that I didn't have to choose. I just had to stop believing that having access to all options meant that something would go wrong as a result. Remember that whole fear of success thing we talked about a few chapters back? The only reason I can write about it with such detail is because I've lived it.

Once I decided that success was safe, having it all became an option, and from there I realized exactly how I could (and how you can) have it all.

YOU CAN HAVE IT ALL.
JUST NOT ALL AT ONCE.

Multi-tasking is for the birds. Show me someone who says that they can multi-task and I'll show you someone who does multiple things poorly. I mean, I get why people think it's a good idea. If you have a lot on your plate, it would stand to reason that if you can manage a few things at a time, you can take care of business much faster. But the thing is, if you split your energy and focus between multiple things at once, it's impossible for any of those things to get 100 percent of you. This applies to your to-do list at work as well as your mission to move past mediocre and take control of your life. You can have it all, BUT you cannot have it all at once. You can't multitask and split your attention between all your pursuits and expect for any of them to go anywhere.

I can't write this book with my daughter on my lap and expect to create a masterpiece while giving my daughter all of my love. If I chose to multitask in this way, I'd likely end up with an ironically mediocre book and a daughter who would grow up to resent my lack of presence with her.

I can be an amazing husband and an incredible coach to my clients, just not in the very same moment. I can't be on date night with my wife and be thinking through how I can help one of the guys I coach. Similarly, it would be unfair to one of my clients if I were distracted by my honey-do list while they were working their way through an emotional breakthrough.

Split energy and focus take away from each party and pursuit involved. The key to having it all is setting boundaries around each thing that you care about, then becoming as present as humanly possible while you're spending time and energy trying to nurture that part of your life.

> THAT ROCK AND HARD PLACE YOU
> FIND YOURSELF BETWEEN ARE
> BOTH FICTIONAL.

If it's date night, be all there.

If you're at work, give it 100 percent of your attention.

If you're at the gym, stop worrying about all the things you have to do after you leave the gym.

If you're spending time with your kids, put your phone down and actually be in the room.

When you become present and intentional with each thing that you want to create or grow in your life, you will literally be able to have it all. You may not want girls on bread like our friend Joey Tribbiani, but you probably want to have a beautiful marriage, an awesome career, and a rockin' bod. You're allowed to have each one.

All it takes is a decision that supports this idea. As Henry Ford famously said:

*"Whether you think you can or you think you
can't, you're right."*

If you don't believe you're allowed to have it all,
that's what you'll experience. If, however, you decide
that you get to have a sizable portion of each part of
life's buffet, then it's yours for the taking.

THERE IS NO HARM IN HAVING IT ALL

I promise you that you can have everything you
desire. Your subconscious mind probably started a
riot as you read that sentence, but it's true. However,
if you believe that you can't have it all, one way that
your (disempowering) belief will show up in your life
is a healthy portion of self-sabotage.

In your mind, there's a subconscious rank of all
the things that truly mean something to you. The desire to lose some weight, start a business, or pursue a
romantic relationship could be ignited within you at
any moment, but if you think your pursuit of your
version of happiness will hurt you or someone you
love, you've got no shot.

As I've mentioned, when my daughter was born, I
was trying to juggle a ton. Husband, father, coach,
writer, and teacher were all hats that I wore on any
given day. My conscious mind was trying to figure
out how to make it all work, thinking that I could
have my cake and eat it, too. My subconscious mind,
however, was determined to thwart my plans. Every

time I got a hit of what life coaching was like, I would somehow take a step or two backwards. I'd sign a client or two, get hyped up with enthusiasm, and then stall out for a few months at a time. It didn't make any sense to me.

But now that I know my subconscious mind on a more personal level, I realize that it was attempting to (inaccurately) inform me that I couldn't have it all while steering me back toward what I valued most: being a husband and father. When push comes to shove, my wife and my daughter are my everything. If even the slightest part of me ever thought that I was giving up time with them to pursue my passion as a coach, I would sabotage the coaching opportunity in favor of quality time with them. Underneath it all, I thought that my success as a coach would do harm to everything else I held close to my heart.

But let me tell you something, my friend. Not only is your success in all things safe for you and yours, it is imperative. Shying away from what you want in this life and playing small is a surefire way to bury resentment deep within you. Do you really think you can be the best partner, parent, or person you can be if you're not fulfilled by the life that you live? When you are whole, your world and all that you touch within it benefits.

Once I realized that my itch to serve my clients was as valuable to me as it was to my family, my business took off. As I stepped into my power as a coach, I became more fulfilled as a person, allowing me to give my wife and daughter a better version of who I was. My success didn't (and hasn't) cost me anything. In fact, it's made everything better.

People who say you can't have it all are just bitter because they chose to play small. They will love telling you that you're not realistic and that you're a dreamer. Pay them no mind. Being realistic is for chumps. Let them run on autopilot as they create a life that they're only halfway happy about. You don't have to follow in their footsteps. Now that you understand the depths of your subconscious mind, you also understand that it's been fooling you the whole time. You get to have it all. You get to be in love with your life. You don't have to settle for anything less than everything you dream of.

It's safe to pursue your version of success. Just set some boundaries, be present in every moment that you're living, and trust that you're not harming your happiness or anyone else's by going after a life that sets you on fire.

Buckle up. Life's about to get really fun.

PART 2

Getting from Subconscious to
Conscious, Intentionally

I just went on and on for a while about the subconscious mind in hopes that you could become more aware of the inner workings of the head games you play with yourself. It's my hope that, by now, you have a decent sense of what thoughts have become automatic, what beliefs have been trapped under the surface, and what actions have been at the mercy of the beast that is your subconscious mind.

Being aware of the gifts and curses of your subconscious mind is super important, but if I simply leave you more aware of the power under the hood of your mind, I'm only doing half the job. It's time to find out how to access your subconscious mind, bring all of those deep, ingrained traits into the limelight, and figure out what to do with them all.

This section of the book will be briefer than the one preceding it as well as the one that follows, but don't skip past it because of its brevity. In this section

I will give you the keys that will unlock your subconscious mind. This is where we'll build the bridge between your subconscious patterns and your conscious control of them, allowing you to shift and transform anything that might stand in your way.

With these tools you'll be able to pull back the curtain of your subconscious, allowing you to consciously make the changes that will keep you moving past mediocrity.

Let's do this.

Chapter 9

Time to Wake Up

The first part of this book has been dedicated to *what* is going on in your subconscious mind. My hope is that it brought you some awareness and allowed you to see the amazing power that sits just below the surface of your skull. Thinking about the way that you think can be a trippy experience, but knowing why you believe that "money doesn't grow on trees" or why you fear failure and success equally is essential to making any changes for the better. Now that you know what's going on upstairs, let's tap into *how* to get in there and get your hands dirty.

Knowing what your subconscious mind can do for you—both good and bad—is a great start, but if we stop there, our work will be incomplete. That would feel about as good as a doctor sitting you down in his office, telling you all about the infectious disease that lives inside you, and then deciding not to follow all the doom and gloom with solutions.

I won't do you like that.

Your subconscious thoughts and beliefs aren't a disease, but they are infectious. Whatever is baked into your brain will permeate into everything you see, hear, and feel as you walk through life. There's a good chance that you have some awesome habits and patterns of behavior that are running on autopilot. There's also a pretty good chance that you also have some self-destructive tendencies residing between your ears.

No matter the ratio between the habits that build you up and the ones that break you down, it would be nice if you could get in there and have a say as to what stays and what goes. The power of the subconscious mind is infinite, but not having any access to it isn't all that fun. It's like having billions of dollars sitting in the bank but not being able to spend a dime.

This chapter will give you three ways to open the door to your subconscious mind. That's right, I'm giving you access to the billion dollars' worth of brain bucks that have been lying dormant for eons. If you apply these three concepts in your life consistently, you'll be able to turn the tides of your subconscious and create shifts in your life that you never thought possible. Let's begin, shall we?

MEDITATION

Comedian Jim Gaffigan is probably most well-known for his take on all things food, but in his stand up special, *Beyond The Pale,* Gaffigan takes an intentional turn down an awkward street and riffs on all things Jesus. As Gaffigan points out during his bit, the mere mention of J.C. makes most people uncomfortable. He even jokes that the Pope likely gets a little squeamish when Jesus is brought up out of context: *"Eaaaaassy buddy. I keep work at work."*

At one point during the five minutes of Gaffigan's hilarious perspective on religion, he offers the throwaway comment, "There's nothing like a Jesus joke to take the air out of the room." Whether it was a joke or an in-depth chat, you've experienced this before, I'm sure. Mr. Christ gets tossed into conversation, and everyone gets quiet. Even mentioning plans of going to church can make some people feel uncomfortable. You may even feel a little unsettled with all the Jesus talk throughout just the last few paragraphs of this book. Don't worry, I won't be quoting Bible verses or anything moving forward.

My point is that Jim's accurate take on the discomfort and awkward silence that religion can bring to a room is similar to the atmosphere that I've seen the concept of meditation create. Meditation is a spiritual practice by nature, so maybe it just gets lumped into the same general category in some people's minds.

But when I mention that I meditate regularly, some folks run for the conversational hills.

"Oh, that's cool, Nick. I just remembered that I had plans to donate a kidney today. I gotta go…"

Don't get me wrong, it's become more accepted in our culture in recent years with a heavy push for mindfulness in our fast-paced, chronically stressed culture. But it isn't exactly the hot topic at the water cooler. Is that still a thing, by the way? Do people still hang around the water cooler and chat it up like they did in the olden days? *Rein it in, Nick.*

With apps such as Headspace and Calm, more people are meditating and/or talking about meditation than when I began my journey going within. But even with it gaining steam in our culture, many people still don't really get what it's about. The fact of the matter is that mediation isn't something you do simply to earn a spiritual merit badge. We like to stack a bunch of activities and actions on top of each other to make ourselves feel good about all of our hard work over here in the Western world, and meditation has, to a degree, gotten wrapped up in that go-getter culture for some people.

"I totally crushed my meditation this morning, bro. I hit my personal best for time and depth of breath, I'm the best meditator in the city!"

Approaching meditation like that only weakens the practice. Viewing it through the frame of competition and challenge will only take away from its purpose.

There are as many brands of meditation as there are flavors of soda, but none of them are meant to be propped up as a measuring stick for mindfulness.

YOU CAN'T HUSTLE YOUR WAY TO
WHOLENESS, HOMIE.

Want to know how to meditate?

Close your eyes (after you read this paragraph, of course) and, as you breathe in, softly think or say the word "in." As you exhale that breath, softly think or say the word "out." Continue this gentle back and forth of "in" and "out" for as long as you see fit. Whenever your mind wanders—and it will—navigate your thought back to "in" and then "out" and have compassion for yourself along the way.

Don't be discouraged if your mind races and fights your attempt to slow things down, just keep practicing, day-in and day-out. You're essentially slamming the brakes on in a vehicle that's used to operating at

100 mph every moment of every day. You're fighting the laws of inertia: an object that is usually in motion will tend to—and prefer to—stay in motion, so any attempt to slow it down will cause friction. The more you intentionally slow down and find your breath, though, the easier it becomes.

And, for my skepticism junkies, meditation isn't all rainbows, sunshine, and feel good vibes; there's science behind its effectiveness. Much like your mind and its conscious and subconscious playgrounds, your autonomic nervous system—the involuntary controller of your heart rate, blood pressure, and digestion— has two realms in which it operates as well. One of the two zones of operation is called the sympathetic nervous system.

When the sympathetic nervous system is in charge, it's preparing your body to react to stress. It keeps your body alert and aware of any danger that lurks, whether that's a drunk driver who swerves into your lane or your boss on a warpath after a record-low month in sales. This side of your autonomic nervous system can be useful when you need to react swiftly to the stresses of your day. But living in a constant state of fight or flight can be pretty destructive to your overall health. It also doesn't allow for much meta-cognition. There's not a lot of room for thinking about your thought process at either the conscious or subconscious level when you're putting out fires left and right.

You don't think, "I wonder why I snapped at my wife like that. I wonder if it's because I saw my dad do that a lot when I was a kid..." in the middle of your latest quarrel with your spouse, you're just trying to survive and get through it. You don't reflect on your tendency to self-sabotage your financial progress every time you get paid, hit the bar, and run up a tab that would make an Irish drunk blush. When your sympathetic nervous system has the wheel, it calls on your subconscious patterns to do its dirty work. There's no time to think about every little move you make when you're living in a world of reaction, so your subconscious mind pairs perfectly with this sympathetic nervous system. They're a pretty cute couple.

But it's awfully hard to observe something that's constantly on the move. You can't take an objective peek at your subconscious thoughts and beliefs if they're zipping around trying to help you react to stress while your sympathetic nervous system is quarterbacking things.

This is where meditation comes in.

The act of meditating allows you to click into the calmer, slowed-the-eff-down counterpart to your autonomic nervous system—the parasympathetic nervous system. It's not like you become this enlightened being the first time you close your eyes and focus on your breath; you just give your body and mind the opportunity to hit pause for a second. By committing to the practice of meditation, you give yourself the chance to slow things down on a daily basis. This tells your body, "It's all good here, you can relax." Cortisol and adrenaline—the mighty combo of hormones that leave you stressed out with gray hair—take a long lunch break and both your body and mind can power down from their usual states of tension and action.

In terms of accessing and observing your subconscious mind and the way it operates, the parasympathetic is where you want to be. Will you be able to fix your subconscious self-talk right away? Nope. Will you be able to change your subconscious block about money the first time you hit pause? Not a chance. But what you *will* be able to do is see them. Awareness is the first step to transforming anything.

If you don't know what to change, you're going to have an awfully hard time changing it. That sentence may not seem all that important, but it really is. In the physical world around you, if you can observe something with your five senses, you can easily tell when something needs to shift. If I catch a wretched whiff of my daughter's diaper, I know that it needs changing. If I see that a light bulb is out, I don't think twice about switching it out. If I can feel my pants getting a little too snug after some holiday binge eating, I know enough to throw on my sweats. It's child's play, really. If you can smell, see, feel, hear, or taste that something's off, it's not hard to conclude that you have to make some changes.

But you can't see your mind.

Meditation allows you to power down and slip into the parasympathetic nervous system, giving you the best opportunity to see what's going on under all the chatter. Things that have been buried in your subconscious mind for decades might swim to the surface and finally show themselves to you.

Will you experience this grand awakening the first time you sit down and meditate? Absolutely not. Meditation is a *practice*. It takes time to train your body and mind to chill out enough for you to get a clear picture of what's really going on in your head. But with a little patience and some trust, you'll find that meditation can be an amazing access point to your unconscious thoughts and behaviors.

JOURNALING

Just a few paragraphs ago I mentioned that you can't see your mind. Well, journaling is about as close as you are going to get to creating a visual of those thoughts, emotions, and behaviors that were previously unseen. Pairing some form of journaling practice with a consistent meditation practice will optimize your ability to take a peek behind the curtain that cloaks your subconscious mind. It's like watching a movie and then trying to jot down the notes of what you remember.

Let's be clear, though. I was NOT open to journaling in the earlier days of my self-improvement journey. *"I'm a grown man! I'm not keeping a diary."* I put off giving it a go for years because having a conversation or dialogue with myself via a piece of notebook paper felt far too feminine. But fellas, allow me to shoot it to you straight: I missed out on a sizeable amount of transformation due to my ego's resistance to something that felt a little too girly. Now that I write in my journal every single day, I know the power that comes from letting your mind leak onto the page. It's kind of a big deal.

As much as I'd like to continue to wax poetically about journaling and the difference it has made in my life, I know you're not here for that. You want the good stuff. You want to know how to journal your face off and bend your subconscious mind at will. A word of caution before I give you the goods: similar to meditation, the act of journaling will only be weakened if approached from the mindset of the go-getter. The more effort and forceful energy you put into it, the less you'll get out of it. However, if you approach journaling with zero expectations and just be mindful in your practice, you can get a lot out of it.

Although journaling doesn't require any format, I've found that there are two ways you can engage your pen and paper to truly tap into your subconscious mind. The first form of journaling allows you to simply observe your subconscious mind--pull back the curtain, if you will. With that awareness, you can then begin to make changes as you see fit. The second form is one that will allow you to mold your subconscious mind and imprint it with thoughts and visions of what you desire. In both cases, the automatic processes of your unconscious mind will never be the same.

Stream of Consciousness

If "stream of consciousness" seems a little too head-in-the-clouds and hippie-ish for you, think of this form of journaling as a brain dump. When engaging with it, you simply sit with your thoughts and let it rip. You begin writing with no end goal in sight aside from allowing your mind to unload itself onto the page or computer screen.

The point of this brain dump is to empty your mind. On the surface, it may seem like a simple task, but you may find yourself judging or overthinking what you come up with, causing you to get stuck mid-dump. To make the process easy, start small and let it flow from there. Write out your schedule for the day and note what you're excited about. Eventually you'll find a mental door that opens you up to more information that's been waiting to be unleashed. Observe what's in the room around you as you write and riff on what certain items mean to you. Once you create some momentum in the process, you'll reach new levels of consciousness to observe and write about.

Notice that in both of the examples I listed, I suggested that you start with something concrete (your schedule or the objects surrounding you) and then follow with how you feel or what they mean to you. By beginning with tangible pieces of information and then shifting to a deeper, emotional connection to that tangible data, you are bridging the gap between the conscious and subconscious mind. It starts on the surface level and then digs a little deeper, allowing you to chip away at thoughts that you probably don't spend a lot of time with.

With each subconscious door you walk through and each rabbit hole you go down, enter without judgment. Just keep writing.

It's possible that you'll write something down that your conscious and active mind will want to judge or feel guilty about. *"You can't possibly think that about your job. They're so good to you there!"* Just let it flow and see what comes out. There's a good chance that, whether it's purely for release or for honest observation, whatever thought or belief has been trapped below the surface of your mind needs to be brought out of you.

WANT TO KNOW HOW TO JUDGE
YOURSELF (AND
YOUR THOUGHTS) LESS?

GET OFF YOUR HIGH HORSE AND
STOP JUDGING OTHER PEOPLE. IF
YOU THINK YOU'VE RESERVED IT
FOR THE PEOPLE AROUND YOU,
YOU'RE SORELY MISTAKEN. THEY
WERE JUST PRACTICE FOR WHEN
YOU WANTED TO TURN THAT
JUDGMENT ON YOURSELF.

Let it go, let it out, and let it be. Then, once you have your thoughts on paper, study what you've written. You now have a picture of your subconscious mind to play with.

Visualization

Stream of consciousness journaling accesses your subconscious mind in an attempt to see what's going on in the dark corners of your mind. Visualization, however, accesses the subconscious to do something very different: mold it.

By writing down the kind of life you want to create, you begin to tell an emotional story about your desires. As we touched on in Part 1, we all tell ourselves stories about our lives, even when we don't know we're the narrator. When you carve out time to *intentionally* create a story that represents your ultimate success, you can begin to imprint your subconscious mind with the emotions, thoughts, and beliefs that are a part of that vision for your future.

You might have wanted to call bullshit after reading that last paragraph. You might think, *"Creating a fictional story of my future isn't going to change my very real present circumstances."* First, if that's the belief you want to hold onto, then you're right. It won't change your current reality. But, on the off chance that this could actually work—that you could *actually* mold your subconscious mind by visualizing your future and writing down what you want it to look like—isn't it a belief pattern that's worth trying? Wouldn't it be worth a shot? If so, stay with me.

In order to change the programming of your subconscious mind, you have to first speak its language: emotions and vibrations. Talk is very, very cheap when communicating with the subconscious realm of your mind. Your words, your stories, and the messages you send yourself need to carry the weight of meaningful emotion in order to be worth anything. So, when visualizing and crafting your (imperfectly) perfect future, let your emotions get wrapped up in the story. Pinpoint how you would feel if you were living in the moment of all the awesomeness that you've crafted.

THE MORE NATURAL YOUR VISION
FEELS BEFORE IT COMES TO PASS,
THE MORE LIKELY IT IS TO OCCUR.

Once your mind catches the vibe of the story and the emotions that are tied to it, all it needs is some repetition to take hold in your subconscious. Remember, the subconscious mind is the Land of Habit; it cherishes repetition. If you drown your mind in the emotions and vibrations of your imagined future over and over again, you're speaking the right language and taking the right approach for your subconscious mind to welcome your vision with open arms.

Does this mean that you'll wake up next week and your life will resemble what you've written down in your journal? Probably not. This isn't about overnight success or instant transformation. It is about changing the wiring in your mind so that when the opportunity presents itself, you're equipped with the right beliefs, thoughts, and story to move your life toward what you want. The visualization practice is just that--practice.

When you get your reps in on paper, you are simply preparing your mind and body for what you want to have and how you want to feel. That way, when it's go-time in real life, you'll already have a sense of what to do.

HIRE A COACH

Since you're a human being, you've undoubtedly made mistakes in your romantic relationships at some point. Whether choosing the right person to be with or treating the person you chose the right way, you've probably made a misstep or two with a few people. When you pair two imperfect humans together, the probability of one or both parties making a mistake is pretty much 100 percent.

When you're in the thick of the relationship, though, it's hard to know when you're not getting it right. They say that love is blind, but that's only because when you're in the trenches of it all, you're too close to the problem to see that it's a problem. You trip, stumble, and fall over things that you could've avoided if you saw them for what they actually were. Seeing your situation objectively is nearly impossible.

But, when you watch a friend go through their own relationship issues, you can diagnose what's going on from a mile away. The solutions to their problems seem so obvious that you get frustrated when they can't see it as clearly as you do. You just want to shake them and scream about how easily they could fix things. It's not that you know any more about their relationship than you know about your own. It's just that you have the gift of distance, of objectivity. You can only see the patterns and the signs of trouble because you're far enough away from ground zero. They're so wrapped up in the emotions of their circumstances that they can't see what you see from your perspective.

Now, parallel this concept of your objective point of view with accessing—and changing—your subconscious mind.

When it comes to tapping into and altering your subconscious mind, that kind of distance and perspective is an asset. Just like your friend who couldn't quite figure out why his relationship wasn't working, you likely are too close to your own thoughts, beliefs, and patterns of behavior to realize how flawed they are. This is why hiring a coach can be one of the best things you do for yourself as you look to make real lasting changes in your life.

A coach is far enough away from your hang-ups that they can see them clear as day. That distance--paired with their expertise in giving you the tools to solve your problems once they're spotted--creates a tidal wave of change that is much harder to create all on your own. Is it impossible to do it solo? Not at all. It will probably just take you longer to figure it all out without the help and guidance of a well-intentioned coach.

It's like trying to walk cross country vs. flying. Both can get you where you need to go, but making the investment in a plane ticket is going to get you there a hell of a lot faster. If you started walking from New York to LA, you'd eventually get there. Google says it would take thirty-eight days to make the trek, but that's with no bathroom breaks, no sleep, and no getting lost along the way. Would it cost more to buy a plane ticket? For sure. Would every penny be worth it as you arrived in LA a mere six hours after the journey began? Absolutely. Hiring a coach is the equivalent of purchasing a plane ticket to substantial change. It's an investment, but it cuts out all the time you would waste trying to figure things out by yourself.

I may seem a little biased here, considering the fact that I'm a coach. But I would never have transformed my life in a way that allows me to now powerfully give back in this role if I hadn't taken a leap and hired a coach myself. I spent 2016 immersing myself in plenty of books, podcasts, and YouTube videos of the personal development variety. Anything about habit creation, mindset, or manifesting abundance was my jam, and I couldn't get enough. I read books like this one that would give me a spark of inspiration, and from that inspiration I would generate some incremental change in my life. But I still felt like there was more to be had from this whole idea of self-development. Essentially, I was trying to walk cross country without a map. It was a slow progression, and I didn't really know where the hell I was going.

Then I saw an opportunity that could—and eventually did—change my life. Tommy Baker, a guy I had been closely following for a while through his podcast, *Resist Average Academy,* launched a mastermind group that intrigued me. It looked like it may be just what I needed. It was my plane ticket.

This plane ticket of mine cost me (and my family, mind you) $500. Back then, I was a teacher who made a little extra side cash writing for businesses and entrepreneurs who needed help creating more compelling content. If you haven't heard, teaching isn't the most lucrative profession, nor was I making millions of dollars in my freelance writing practice. Put simply, this mastermind coaching opportunity was an uncomfortable financial decision for me, to say the least. But I felt like I was repeatedly banging my head against my own ceiling of potential as I tried to grow and transform on my own. So I sheepishly asked my wife if she'd be cool with me throwing more than our two car payments combined at this thing that I'd never done before. She was a little confused as to what the heck a mastermind was and why I felt I needed to invest in it, but she graciously gave me the green light.

Here's what happened next. Within a month of putting some money on the line, investing in myself and my own personal growth, and really engaging with what Tommy was bringing to the table…

• I recouped seven times the amount of money that I had put on the line at the beginning of the process.

• I went from writing blog posts for myself and others to helping another member of the mastermind write his own book.

• I realized that my truest calling wasn't just to teach math to high school students but also to inspire people young and old to live their most fulfilled life-- one they wake up every day excited about.

Hiring a coach rocked my world. Since hiring Tommy back then, I've invested in myself consistent-ly. But it's not only because it's nice to have someone to talk to and work through stuff with. It's because a coach's gift comes from his or her ability to see your subconscious mind standing in the middle of the room butt naked. A skilled coach's perspective, paired with his or her ability to dig deeper into what they see, is priceless.

> YOUR SUBCONSCIOUS IS A LION,
> AND A (GOOD) COACH IS THE LION
> TAMER. THEY WILL UNDERSTAND
> THE POWER IT HAS, BUT ALSO
> KNOW HOW TO HARNESS IT TO
> YOUR BENEFIT.

We all have subconscious patterns that hold us back, but oftentimes we have no idea that we do or what they are. I've had coaches help me unlock and unleash patterns about parenthood, money, and a ton of other topics that I simply couldn't have unraveled had I not had someone shining a supportive light on them. And now I have the honor of shining that same supportive, life-shifting light on the patterns of my clients.

Meditation and journaling are incredible habits that will swing open doors in your mind you didn't know existed, but hiring a coach is the gold standard of accessing and changing the patterns of your life that don't serve you anymore. Feel like you're stuck in your ways? Hire a coach. Feel like you've hit your ceiling? Hire a coach. Feel like there's more for you to experience here on this big blue ball we're living on? Hire a coach. It's undoubtedly the fastest, most effective way to dig into what's holding you back and transform those roadblocks into a clear, concise path to the life that you've always dreamed of.

If you don't know where to start, don't hesitate to reach out. Maybe I'm the guy who can help shift your life. If not, I'll happily refer you to the people who have helped shape mine. It's truly the greatest gift you can give yourself, your family, and your community at large. Oh, and that pesky subconscious mind of yours, too. In fact, it will benefit the most. Trust me.

PART 3

Conscious Creation Time

Alright, now it's time to have some fun.

In the first part of this book, we took a look at some of the most popular thoughts, beliefs, emotions, and patterns that have been unknowingly running in the background of your life. The second part of the book showed you how to access that subconscious mind of yours so that you can maneuver around those mental obstacles and break the patterns that have kept you stuck in place.

You've been shown the mental shackles that have kept you imprisoned. You've been given a set of keys to set you free. Now it's time to truly move past mediocre—it's time to take conscious action, step into your greatness, create success, and live your most fulfilled life. I know that last sentence was a little heavy on the buzzwords, but there's beauty behind all that buzzin'. Greatness, success, fulfillment...they're all subjective. You get to choose what they each mean to you, and it will undoubtedly look different for every soul attached to each pair of eyes reading these words. Whatever it means to you, I'm cool with it. I just want you to have it already.

> *"Mediocrity doesn't just happen. It's chosen over time through small choices day by day."*
> —Todd Henry

Mediocrity is a choice. Greatness is a choice. One of them is chosen by default (hello, subconscious), and one of them is chosen by design. You don't just trip and stumble into a life that makes you miserable, nor do you wake up one morning in the middle of a life that you've always dreamt of. In either case, the life that you have and the person who stares you down in the mirror are merely the culmination of a bunch of decisions.

So, what you choose to do today and every day moving forward matters. Make those choices consciously. Make them knowing that your subconscious will pop up from time to time and say something like, "I know you're really excited about this, but I'm not sure if it's safe!" as it tries to shrink you back to the person you don't want to be anymore.

Before reading this book, you may have listened to that message. You don't have to anymore. You don't have to keep choosing what's familiar simply because it's "safe." You can keep moving toward the life that you want despite the whispers of fear that creep up from the subconscious. At the conscious level, you now know that you'll be fine. In fact, you're going to be better than fine as you continue to navigate in the direction of your dreams.

It's time to become a conscious creator. Are you ready?

Chapter 10

Rule #1 as a Conscious Creator: Take Responsibility

The amount of control you have over your life and how it plays out will directly correlate with the amount of responsibility you're willing to take on.

When I was about ten, I made my first All-Star team as a little leaguer. I wasn't the best of the best by any means, but it was cool to land on the roster. While playing on the team, I met a kid named Tom. Through a ton of time spent together both on and off the field that summer, a bromance bloomed. In the years that followed, there weren't many days when we weren't playing home run derby at my house or Xbox at his. We ended up playing ball together every summer in some capacity until we were about nineteen. When we grew up (numerically, anyway) and decided to get hitched to the ladies in our lives, we exchanged turns of being each other's best man. We were, and still are, best friends.

As we've grown older, gotten married, bought houses, and started families, we'll sometimes wax poetic about those days playing baseball from sunup to sundown, then playing video games until the sun came back up again. Ah, the good ol' days.

We don't play many video games anymore. I haven't thrown or hit a baseball in more than five years. Tom and I don't even spend that much time together these days because I was a sucker who fell for a girl who lives an hour and a half from our hometown, then moved out her way to start our life together. We both have mortgages. We both have bills. We probably also have more worry, anxiety, and stress due to those mortgages and bills.

But I remember one specific conversation that he and I had, one where we were in full-on reminiscing mode. We spoke about how carefree we were and how life was so easy back then. I asked him if he preferred those good ol' days compared to the ones he and I were living at that moment, student loans and all. Given the amount of fun we had back then, you'd think he would go back in a heartbeat. But he said he'd rather be the man, husband, and homeowner that he is today. I couldn't have agreed more.

Why would we both choose all this responsibility over the days when we didn't have to worry about a thing? The answer is easy: control. We have more control over our lives than we ever did back then, and that control is a byproduct of the responsibilities that we've taken on as adults.

When we were kids, we may have had little-to-no responsibility, but our lives essentially ran through our parents. If they couldn't shuttle us back and forth to each other's house, we had no choice but to stay put at our respective homes. If they couldn't afford (or didn't want to shell out money for) a new video game, we couldn't do much about it. If they didn't feel like bringing us to our local amusement park for the day, we had to deal with a day without roller coasters. Our lives were dictated by their choices. All we had in our arsenal was a bit of little boy charm and a ton of "pretty *pleeeease*." Luckily, both sets of parents loved us and had become good friends as well, so it was never really a hard sell.

As adults, we are now the gatekeepers of permission. We don't have to beg our parents to let us do anything because we get to decide what we want to do and when we want to do it. The tradeoff that comes with all of this freedom of choice is no more than a hell of a lot more responsibility. And, although it pairs with a little more mental and emotional weight on our shoulders, we'll gladly take it.

BE THE CEO OF YOUR LIFE

Taking responsibility gives you ownership. My buddy, Tom, and I gladly take on our fair share of responsibilities so that we can be the owners and operators of our lives. Our parents used to run the show, but now we're the CEOs of our own day-to-day operations.

If you think about this analogy in the context of business, there are plenty of people who want nothing to do with being a CEO. Sure, the fat paycheck and corner office that overlooks the ocean are nice perks, but many would still opt for the cubicle with a view of the parking lot and a paycheck that barely keeps food on the table. Why? Because when you're the CEO, all the responsibility falls on your shoulders. If business is growing, you're a hero, but if the numbers start moving in the wrong direction, it's your fault. Every decision that comes across your desk is a big one, and if you make the wrong call, the entire landscape of the business can shift. There's a reason that the CEO's paycheck has a few more zeroes at the end of it than that of the guy who spends his day strategically setting up his fantasy football lineup on the company's time. When you're responsible for the success or failure of everything around you, you get to be rewarded for that level of ownership.

It's easier to be a mid-level employee. When business slows, you can point fingers from your cubicle. When layoffs occur, you can blame the executives on the thirty-fifth floor for dropping the ball. It's not your fault that your buddy with the wife and three kids got canned, so you can rest easy at night while complaining about the bigwigs who let your pal go. When problems aren't yours to solve, life ain't so bad. You just show up, punch the clock, and wait until 5:00 pm to sprint out the door.

When paralleled back to your own life, the mindset of a mid-level employee will trap you in a life of mediocrity. You'll just go through the motions. You'll blame other people when things go wrong. You'll give away your power to make any positive change because you feel like the world "is what it is," and you're just along for the ride.

POINTING THE FINGER WON'T SOLVE YOUR PROBLEMS. UNLESS YOU'RE STANDING IN FRONT OF A MIRROR, THAT IS.

But the troubling part is, since you're an adult and all, you're the CEO of your life by default. You were given that title the moment you got your own health insurance, moved out of your parents' house, or started working at your first job that didn't have a food court attached to it. You're the head honcho whether you like it or not. But if you're not willing to take on the responsibilities that come with the gig, you're going to end up running the business that is You, Inc. straight into the ground.

Could you imagine if the CEO of a Fortune 500 company showed up to work and didn't feel like taking on all of the responsibility that came with his job? Picture him twiddling his thumbs at his large desk made of oak, just waiting for someone else to take care of everything for him. How long would it be before that company's stock crashed? Things would go downhill fast.

Responsibility equals results and rewards. If you want the level of your life's results to change, you first need to take more responsibility. Now, what exactly should you take responsibility for, you might ask? Anything and everything, but let's start with the end in mind.

OWN YOUR CURRENT RESULTS

Take a look at your life and observe what the current reality is in all the major buckets within it. How's your relationship going? Are you on the right career path? When was the last time you exercised on purpose (because, admit it, sometimes you walk up the stairs just a little too fast and can count that as cardio)? How is your spirituality and your connection to something bigger than yourself?

Be as objective as humanly possible, and then, when you've painted the picture of what your life currently looks like, understand this: **it's all your fault.** It doesn't matter if your circumstances are good, bad, or somewhere in between. Take responsibility for *all of it*.

The rational side of your brain is going to try and find a scapegoat for pieces that you may feel aren't up to par.

"But my dad was always verbally abusive when I was a kid, so my fear of authority (and my inability to stand up to my prick of a boss) comes from those childhood experiences with my dad."

That's not gonna fly here. You can't point the finger while simultaneously taking ownership of your life. You have to pick a side. In order to shift your life in this moment, you have to let go of being a victim to everything that has led up to it. Leaving the door open to excuse yourself from the part you played in your current circumstances will only make it that much harder to change any of it.

Peel back the layers of your life's onion and examine the role you *had* in the life you *have*. Own up to what you could have done differently in your career, how you could communicate better in your relationship, or how eating a pint of ice cream every night may not be the best thing for that waistline of yours. This isn't a shame and blame party; there's no judgment. I simply want you to take a step back and acknowledge that you had some say in what you're currently experiencing. If your life hasn't played out the way that you wanted, taking this level of responsibility may feel disempowering. But, in reality, by looking back and saying, "I had something to do with this," you can begin to look forward and know that you can have a say in how things evolve from here.

Now, you may have some resistance to this if you've had some objectively bad shit happen to you. If you lost a parent to cancer or a friend was hit by a car and died, you might have some choice four letter words for me right now. How can you take responsibility for something so terrible or own the ripple effect it's had on your life? Before you go biting my head off, hear me out.

You're not at fault for the event itself, but you *are* the only person who's had access to your inner playbook since then. You've had a say in how that event has affected your life since that moment in time.

Your parents' divorce isn't your fault, but the way you've allowed it to affect your relationships with other people is yours to own.

You can't blame yourself if a friend decided to commit suicide, but you can take responsibility for what you made that mean about your life moving forward.

You shouldn't bear the weight of childhood trauma because you were just a kid. But now that you're an adult, investigate and own up to how you've brought that trauma with you.

Do you need to take this level of ownership when you're in the thick of these tragedies? Absolutely not. There is a time and place for grief and sadness, and those emotions need to be felt. But if time has passed and you're ready to lift that burden, taking responsibility for how and why you've carried that emotional weight up to this point will play a key role in loosening the grip that it has on you.

No matter your current circumstances, you can always connect the dots backward and see patterns and behaviors that played a role in the outcome. You know that cliché phrase, "It's not the cards you're dealt; it's how you play the hand"? It's over referenced and overused (and I am fully aware of the irony occurring within this sentence as I, too, just referenced it), but it's true. Clichés are funny like that. At some point, they were beautiful pieces of wisdom, and after going through the ringer of usage, they became a bumper sticker you slap on your Kia.

But it's factual: the cards you're dealt are not your call. How you play them—and the outcome that falls in your lap as a result of that strategy—is what you can take responsibility for.

OWN EACH THOUGHT, BELIEF, AND ACTION MOVING FORWARD

Taking responsibility for how you navigated to your current station in life is only part of the equation. If you stop there, the objective of consciously owning your life is incomplete. You don't want to be caught in the loop of letting life happen to you and then reflecting in reverse on all the things you could have done differently. In order to take back your power to create a life that's far from mediocrity, you need to take responsibility for *everything* moving forward.

Every thought that pops into your head is yours to accept or deny. Every belief that you feel in your bones begins and ends with you. Every action that you take as a result of those thoughts and beliefs also falls on your shoulders.

In the first part of this book, we talked about how some of these things—beliefs in particular—may have been birthed from your observation of your parents, your environment, and the world around you when you were young and impressionable. When you love your parents and respect your teachers, you tend to take their word as gospel. Hell, you're too young to explore anything different anyway.

When you're seven years old, you don't have the mental capacity to ponder your parents' mindset about money and think thoughts such as, "It's interesting that Mom and Dad keep talking smack about rich people but would also love to become one of them. Seems like a conflict of interest." When you're in the first grade, you don't have the wherewithal to think through your aunt's, uncle's, or teacher's thoughts on politics, social issues, or how to live life to the fullest.

Now, none of these people are talking directly to your impressionable mind about these very adult topics (at least, I hope not). But since you're a human and have a pair of working ears, you hear stuff. Back then, you didn't question much of it, and no one could blame you. But now that you're older and you're looking to shape the course of the rest of your life, you can't play victim anymore. It's not your parents' fault that you've let some of those beliefs go unchecked. It's not your little league coach's fault that you haven't revisited all the things you learned from him as a painfully awkward eight-year-old center-fielder.

> YOU MAY NOT HAVE PLANTED THE
> POISONOUS SEED OF BELIEF IN
> YOUR FERTILE BRAIN, BUT NO
> ONE'S GOING TO TEND TO THAT
> CURRENT GARDEN OF WEEDS
> BUT YOU.

Nobody has a say in how you think, feel, believe, or act moving forward. The more that you try to pass off responsibility for how you're operating right now as well as in the days and weeks to come, the more personal power you're donating to the world around you. And the more power you give away to other people, the more hopeless the idea of living your best life will become.

DON'T HOPE FOR CHANGE, MAKE IT A HABIT

If you can't beat 'em, join 'em. If you want to consciously make changes in your life, you're going to have to commit to a subconscious game: habit creation. You can't just wake up one day and hope for a better life; you have to start doing something about it on a consistent basis. Getting all hopped up on the feel-good vibes of living your best life is cool, but as the Greek poet, Archilochus, once said, "You don't rise to the level of your expectations, you fall to the level of your training." You have to *train* yourself to habitually think, feel, and act a certain way. You have to be intentional about it, because when life serves up a few shit sandwiches, you will always fall to your baseline of habit. It's your responsibility to steer the ship of patterns and behaviors. Once you own that responsibility while consciously and consistently taking the reins back from your subconscious mind, your life will change forever.

Habitual Thought

If you've read a personal development book or two in your day, you've probably been shamed into thinking that you have to wake up earlier than everyone else to be a badass in life. There's definitely value in waking up early and getting your day started in the stillness of a quiet morning, but I think that it's not *when* you wake up but *how* you wake up that truly matters. It's 4:49 am as I type this sentence, but the time on the clock when my alarm went off wasn't nearly as important as what happened moments after the sound of said alarm woke me from my slumber.

Before I let my feet hit the floor every morning, I pause to reflect on what I'm grateful for. I won't let myself get out of bed until I've come up with three unique things that I consciously appreciate. It doesn't matter how badly my bladder is screaming at me, I will not leave the warmth of my bed until I have paid homage to three awesome things in my life. Everything from the minute to the monumental is fair game when my eyes first open every morning. Sometimes I'm grateful for the fact that I get to have coffee soon. Sometimes I'm struck by a loving appreciation for my wife and my daughter and the joy they bring to my life. Objectively, those two pieces of gratitude are vastly different in size and scope, but that's not the point. The point is to set the tone for how I want to think as I start my day.

Most of us get up and immediately start to recall what stresses us out or gives us anxiety. Bills, tasks, and to-do lists flood our brain as we rise into a conscious state, crippling our ability to start the day with any form of positivity. But that's just our subconscious reaction to starting the day. You can make a conscious choice to think differently as the day begins to unfold.

The things you do and choose to believe all come from the basis of thought. If you can control your thoughts and steer them in a direction that favors your life, you will hit the ground running rather than stumble through stress from the jump. It may seem like this little practice is too simple, but there is power in its simplicity.

Your energy will always create your experience. If you take responsibility for the first few thoughts that creep into your noggin in the morning and point them toward gratitude, you will begin your day with a momentum of energy toward things you are grateful for. On the opposite end of the spectrum, though, if you start your day on the default human mode of thought, "What can I do today to not die?" you will get the snowball rolling toward an experience of pure survival.

If you'd like to thrive rather than just survive, creating a simple habit around your first thoughts of the day is one of the best things you can do for yourself. Once you start enough days with this practice of gratitude, you'll see why something so simple has the power to shift your life.

Habitual Action

> *"We are what we repeatedly do. Excellence, therefore, is not an act but a habit."*
> —Aristotle

A school I taught at once started an initiative to improve the culture in the building. One of the things they chose to do was create a bulletin board of inspiring quotes in one of the main hallways in hopes that students and staff would see the messages and reflect on how they applied to our mission of improving the way we all interacted with each other.

The first quote they threw up on the board was the one above from Aristotle. I'm a bit of a bookworm and love myself some Greek philosophy, so I remember thinking, "That's awesome! A great quote to set the tone for the messages to follow."

That quote sat alone on the board all year long. What started with good intentions fizzled out almost as quickly as it began. If the English teachers had any sense, they would've used this bulletin board to show their students a concrete example of irony!

Whether it's a school initiative, your hopes of losing weight, or your goal of making more money for your family, not much is going to happen if there aren't habitual actions undertaken in favor of it.

Similar to your thoughts, you can't sit and wait for your actions to become more positive and powerful; you need to make a conscious choice for a shift to occur. Once you've decided to be more intentional with your actions, lean heavily on Aristotle and his quip about doing so repeatedly.

Starting your day with gratitude is an excellent habit to build around your thought patterns because it sets a foundation for what will rattle around in your head throughout the day. Once your feet hit the floor, having a morning routine to guide your actions in a positive way will be equally important as you look to create amazing things in your life. Choosing to do just a few impactful things before you rush off to work or slump into the couch for some Saturday morning cartoons can make the difference between staying in a mediocre slump and building your dream life.

Now, what are those few magical activities that you can build into your repertoire to take hold of your morning, giving you ownership of your day and, consequently, your life? You have to meditate for thirty minutes, read four books, run ten miles, do 1,000 pushups, and then journal until your pen runs out of ink. Then and only then will you become an extraordinary human being.

I'm kidding.

This doesn't have to be complicated. In fact, the more complex your attempts at building these habits become, the less likely you'll stick to the process. It's important that you keep things simple enough that it makes it easy to show up and perform every single day.

When I work with my coaching clients, the morning routine that we put into place ensures that they take care of their mind, body, and soul.

• They move their **body** and get in some exercise bright and early. Whether it's yoga or powerlifting, getting the blood pumping shortly after waking up is nature's cup of coffee.

• They engage their **mind** with content that will spark insights or open new lines of thought that they haven't been exposed to. Sometimes it'll be a book on stoicism, other times it's a podcast on personal development principles.

• Finally, they give intentional time to their **soul** with a form of meditation of their choice. Sitting in silence is the gift of calm that we all could use before we're met with the noise of the day.

This morning ritual doesn't have to (nor should it) become a two-hour long saga. Start small and keep it simple. Allot fifteen minutes to each facet of the routine, and let it flow naturally into the beginning of your day. Move your body, engage your mind, nourish your soul.

Take conscious responsibility for the things you do first thing in the morning, and you'll be surprised by how easy it becomes to choose actions that serve you most throughout the day. By putting this morning routine in place and allowing it to become a habit, you'll be setting yourself up for positive momentum to start each day. Not only that, you'll also be putting that momentum on cruise control. Wouldn't it be nice to put something that brings value to your life on autopilot in place of all of the patterns we uncovered in the first part of this book? I figured you might be on board with that.

Habitual Belief

The results that you allow yourself to experience in life can only rise as high as the level of belief you have in yourself and what you believe you deserve. Many of us think that circumstances such as where we live, the family we were born into, or the job we have are the constraints with which the world ties us down. But, in reality, the only thing tying us down and keeping us anchored to the things we don't want in life is belief.

Take money and wealth, for instance. About one percent of the humans walking this earth have over a million dollars in assets. As much as some of us would love to throw stones at these people, creating a story of how greedy they are and how they take advantage of the middle and lower classes, they haven't made their fortunes out of a pure sense of evil. They've stacked their cash because they believed they were worthy and deserving of that kind of wealth. Have you ever felt weird about asking for or being gifted money? You know, you get a little pit in your stomach as the money exchanges hands while you quietly consider whether you should accept the transaction? Wealthy people don't have that problem--at least not in a way that would hold them back from accumulating large sums of money. They have an inner belief that the cash that's coming their way is something they're worthy of, therefore they don't—and shouldn't—feel badly about accepting the offering.

Your bank account isn't the only place where belief and worthiness are the gatekeepers of success, either. You won't be able to get (and stay) in shape until you believe that you're worthy of that level of health. You won't find life-changing love until you believe that you're worthy of that kind of connection with someone else. In health, wealth, and happiness, you will always get what you think you deserve. No more, no less.

Because of this, it's crucial to consciously check in with yourself and take responsibility for what you believe. You can't float through life without observing what you think you're capable of and expect your life to magically transform into something that lights you up. You have to habitually look deep inside your heart and soul and see what patterns of belief you've been hanging onto.

Just like starting your day with thoughts of gratitude and a simple morning routine of action, creating a consistent practice around getting curious about what you believe is the key to being able to create positive change.

So, how do you dig into your patterns of belief and see them for what they are? **You need to voluntarily look at the areas of your life in which you feel limited.**

They're called *limiting* beliefs for a reason. There are things that you think, feel, and believe about your life that are keeping you stuck. But if you don't consciously and consistently take a look at those limitations, you'll never know what's *really* getting in your way.

Once a week, carve out twenty minutes to write down anything and everything that you feel has been a challenge as of late. If your bank account is feeling slim, write it down. If your marriage has grown stagnant, put it on the paper. If your job is a soul sucking waste of your adult years, make room to acknowledge it. Then, once a few challenging circumstances are written in black and white, begin to jot down all the reasons why you think you're stuck.

Why are you limited financially? Is it because you're at a dead-end job? Is it because you don't have enough experience to ask for a raise? Is it because you don't have a budget and are spending recklessly?

What's made your marriage become a ghost of what it once was? Is it that your kids got in the way of the quality time you and your spouse spend together? Is it your in-laws? Is it because one of you works long hours and is exhausted when you get home?

Why is your job the bane of your existence? Is it because you're overqualified? Is it because you engage in the same monotonous tasks over and over again? Is it because you work too many hours for the salary you've agreed to?

Spend some time getting curious about why you're stuck, frustrated, and spinning your wheels. Once you've filled your paper with all the reasons why you're struggling, do one of two things:

• **Call bullshit.** Get honest with yourself and call out whatever isn't really true. There's a good chance that some of your reasons point the finger at someone else or blame something outside of yourself for your challenges. Is it *really* that you don't have enough experience to ask for a raise, or is it just that you're scared? Is it *really* that your marriage is on the rocks because of how much you have to work, or do you just avoid coming home because you don't want to deal with the real issues in your relationship? Get real. Get honest. The more you can take responsibility here, the more control you'll have when it comes to shifting these beliefs.

• **Take care of the easy stuff.** There's likely something super simple that you've been putting off that could be the difference maker when it comes to your limitation. Take budgeting, for instance. If your cash flow has become a problem, take the uncomfortable action of sitting down and looking at where you're spending your money and how much you're bringing in. Sometimes, it's not about having a huge realization about a deep-seated belief but instead doing something simple despite it not being all that fun.

Abraham-Hicks is famous for saying that a belief is simply a thought that you keep thinking. The problem is that many of us don't take the time to observe what we're thinking about and how true or untrue those things might be. Taking the time to lay it all out and sift through your mind once a week will allow you to see those beliefs and repeated thoughts with your own eyes. Once you see what's going on in your mind, you have more freedom to change those beliefs and can begin to think thoughts that will move you forward instead.

HOW RESPONSIBLE HAVE YOU BEEN?

Taking full responsibility for both the efforts you put into your life and the outcomes that show up as a result gives you more control over your life than you've ever had. Before you quickly lick your thumb and use the added traction to flip to the next page, pause and think about how much ownership you've taken in your life. How often do you point the finger? How often do you donate your power to choose your thoughts, beliefs, and actions to someone else?

Become aware of where you need to raise your level of responsibility in life. The more ownership you choose to take, the more power you'll have to steer your life in the direction that you desire.

Chapter 11

Do More of What You're Good At

I am not a handyman.

There are some guys who look around their house and dream up what they could create with their bare hands. Maybe they want to build their own bar or have some other DIY project in mind. I, on the other hand, sit back and hope that nothing breaks, because I would have no idea how to fix it. YouTube has taught me some helpful skills such as how to screw in a lightbulb (I'm only sort of kidding). My skills with a power drill max out at hanging up various things around the house, and I'm not even that great at that. I've left a few botched holes in the wall in my should-be-in-front-of-a-computer-screen wake.

I used to struggle (really, my ego used to struggle) with my lack of skill with hammers, nails, and anything else you might find in a toolbox. The two men that are closest to me are quite the opposite. My dad is a MacGyver of sorts, always finding unique ways to solve problems with whatever resources he has. I'm pretty sure he once patched up a hole in the muffler of my car with a Coors Light can. How, you ask? If I knew how he used a can of not-so-great beer to fix my car, I probably wouldn't be telling you all about my supreme lack of handiness, would I? I just know that one day I started my car, and it didn't sound like a machine gun was going off as I drove. All thanks to my dad and the magic of the Silver Bullet. My father-in-law also knows his way around the work bench. He literally makes his own furniture. And then there's me, the guy who once Googled "blinker fluid" to see if it's something I should ask the mechanic to check on my car. That's not a cute little quip; that actually happened.

With each checkpoint of manhood—moving out of my parents' house, getting married, having a kid, and so on—I became increasingly anxious about my ineptness in all things handy. I thought, *How in the world can I be enough as a husband or a father if I can't unclog the garbage disposal?*

But, as it turns out, my ability to excel as a husband and father—the two things that matter the most to me—have little to do with my ability to fix things. My wife won't love me less if I can't change the brakes on her car. My daughter won't hate me if I can't build her a dollhouse from scratch. They jus need me to keep showing up as who I am, and who I am is *not* Mr. Fix It. Will I learn some things along the way, as we all do through life experience? Of course I will. But I don't need to go out of my way to become an encyclopedia of craftsmanship knowledge.

> THE BUMMER IS NEVER THE FACT THAT YOU CAN'T FIT INTO THE SOCIETAL BOX YOU THOUGHT YOU NEEDED TO EXIST IN. IT STEMS FROM THE FEELING THAT YOU HAVE TO BE THERE IN THE FIRST PLACE.

Both you and I owe the world the greatest expression of our truest selves. Anything less than that would be a shame. But so many of us get caught up doing things, learning things, and spending time with things that don't matter. The law of conservation of energy in physics and chemistry states that energy can neither be created nor destroyed, it simply remains constant. Putting this in terms of *your* energy—both physical and mental—you are prescribed a certain amount of it. You can't get more. You can't get less.

In other words, you need to use it wisely. If you're devoting a ton of energy toward something that doesn't serve your greater good, that means it's energy that you don't get to use for something you love, are good at, or simply find joy in.

Every minute that I've scrolled through YouTube or scoured the internet for answers to my questions about fixing something was a minute that I didn't give to something I am good at and passionate about. That energy was misplaced on something I had little desire to become great at when it could have been put toward something that would create a larger impact on my life. If I deeply desired to become either of the handymen I look up to, that time and energy spent studying the craft would be well worth it. But I'd rather spend that time and energy writing books like this one and becoming the best coach that I can be for my awesome clients.

So now, instead of investing more time and energy toward hammers and nails, I simply invest some money in a contractor or an expert who can take care of those projects for me. This may seem like I'm just throwing money at the problem rather than learning to solve it. If that's the case, I'm going to run into some trouble when we run out of money and I need an oil change or our laundry machines are on the fritz. But rather than entertaining that rabbit hole of scarcity, let me offer you a different perspective. By giving more of my time and attention to the things that I love to do and have a set of skills in, I get to become the greatest and truest version of who I am. When I operate from that state, I can make way more money than I would if I used that time and energy to learn more about fixing toilets, patching up roofs, or replacing the brakes on my car. With more money flowing into my life, paying someone else to take care of things that I'm not good at is a no-brainer because it allows me to spend that time getting even better at my craft. It's a win-win when you double down on what you're good at, trust me.

JACK OF ALL TRADES...MASTER OF NONE

This book is all about moving past mediocre and fighting the tides of average that so many of us get bogged down in. In order for you to rise above the mediocrity that the general population likes to wade through, it's imperative that you stop listening to the narrative that says you need to become a well-rounded human. Look, I'm not saying that you should cut out all activities that don't involve your passions, but if you find yourself spending a lot of mental and physical energy on stuff that doesn't serve your life's purpose, find ways to trade some of that time and attention for more of what you love.

If you have the drive to be a world-class dancer, dedicating a substantial amount of time and energy to learning about the stock market is a waste of time. Putting some money in the market isn't a bad idea, but there's also someone you can pay to take care of that for you. If you have deep desires to be the best baker in your town, getting caught up in YouTube tutorials on how to setup your website will draw you away from where your attention is needed: the baking. Having a flawless website won't mean jack if your cupcakes are dry.

To give you a tangible example from my own life, at this very moment there is a guy outside of my house plowing the snow out of my driveway for me. We live just outside of Rochester, NY, and the fluffy white stuff comes to visit us quite often. When we bought our house, we needed to make a decision about how to handle the inevitable blizzard conditions and the mess it would leave behind in our driveway.

Our choices? Buy a snowblower or hire someone to plow our driveway for us. In the long run, it would be far cheaper to opt for the snowblower, but here I am writing to you from the warmth of my office while some guy with a big truck cleans up our driveway for us. So, why go the more costly route? Because if we bought a snowblower, I would have to rise well before the sun to get our driveway clear before I leave for work. It would require that I spend those early morning hours playing in the snow instead of reading, writing, meditating, and exercising. The early morning hours are when I do my best work, and without using them wisely, my business wouldn't exist, I'd for sure be rocking a dad bod, and this book would merely be something I'd like to create "someday."

Could I have bitten the bullet, bought the snowblower, and just sucked it up on the mornings that it snowed? Of course I could have. In fact, many probably would have considered that the sensible approach. It's not like it snows everyday here during the winter. But from where I sit (a warm office), giving ALL of my mornings to things that I'm passionate about and good at is so much more valuable than dividing my attention and intention in any way.

The sensible answer is often the one that keeps you living the average life you're trying to escape, because the sensible answer is the one that most people would approve of. If the majority of the crowd is in favor of the way that you're operating, you're destined to land in the middle of that same crowd.

The crowd wants you to be well-rounded. The crowd thinks that you should work on your weaknesses. The crowd believes that it's a rite of passage for adults to learn how to handle all of the "adult" things that exist in life (taxes, house repair, bills, etc.).

I say, *To hell with all that*.

If you are a jack of all trades, that means you've too generously divided your attention to those trades. It means you're not as great as you could have been at the one thing you were supposed to be absolutely world class at doing.

If you want to be extraordinary, you need to embrace the conscious decision to take the road less travelled. Your pie chart of time and energy shouldn't be divided up evenly; only the activities that will serve your highest self deserve the biggest slice. I'm talking, like, "selfishly taking half of Granny's homemade pumpkin pie on Thanksgiving" type of serving size. Whenever you feel like you're being pulled from your path to greatness, find a way to cut ties with what's sucking time and energy from what you're here to accomplish. Pay someone to file your taxes. Find someone to cut your lawn. Throw money at anything that will give you more time to double down on your craft. Because if you get really good at something, people will pay you so handsomely that whatever cash you tossed around to solve your problems will seem minuscule by comparison.

I am not a handyman. But I'm a damn good writer, coach, and teacher. I'm a world-class husband and father. And as I have gotten better and better in all of my areas of greatness, the more I've consciously made the choice to go all in on what I'm passionate about. I couldn't care less about the ins and outs of fixing the bathroom sink, so I choose to not give it my energy. I've got more important things to take care of.

You have more important things to take care of, too. There is undoubtedly something that comes to mind as you read this chapter about being unapologetically committed to things you're good at and care about. There may be a part of you that wants to shut that voice up. You may think that it's unreasonable not to spend time weed whacking or doing your laundry. If you have the ability to do it, why have someone else do it for you, right?

Because the person you pay to take care of your busy work can likely do it just as well as you can, if not better. But there is no one in the world who can paint like you, write like you, or study and teach nutrition like you. Give your energy and attention to the activities that will serve you and everyone else at the highest level.

Being well-rounded is overrated. Instead, be lopsided in favor of your genius.

Chapter 12

Feel Your Feelings, Dammit

I have been somewhere between knee and waist deep in personal development content for about five years now. I love the high that I get from new insights I get from books, podcasts, or conversations with my mentors. I've learned so much about myself, my view of the world, and what I want to accomplish while I'm still breathing, creating a life that I didn't think was possible prior to my journey down the rabbit hole of all things self-improvement.

One of the people who has taught me the most has never written a book. She doesn't have a podcast or a YouTube channel full of videos dripping with wisdom. In fact, as of this writing, she has yet to say her first word, let alone give a speech on how to live your best life. She's cute. She's funny. She's the pride and joy of the Matiash household. She's my little daughter, Lucy.

Parenting presents this interesting paradox. You do your best to raise these little humans, learning a ton about yourself and life in general along the way. Then, as they get older, you attempt to pass down all the wisdom you've accumulated. You know, the wisdom with roots firmly planted in figuring life out while raising those once-little humans. In my limited experience, being a parent has been the best education I've received yet.

Once Lucy was born, class was in session.

One of the biggest lessons that she's taught me is with regard to how important and healthy it is to experience your emotions and let them flow through you, no matter whether they're positive or negative. I was an emotional guy before she ever came along; my wife has lovingly called me a sap on numerous occasions. But Lucy has tugged at my heart and torn up my gut in ways that have forced me to come face to face with many feelings I previously may have tried to choke down.

These days she's an absolute joy to be around, but in the first few months of her life, she was a real handful. She was content roughly 0.0001 percent of the time, making for long days filled with attempts at soothing her followed by long nights hoping we could all finally get some sleep. My wife and I were in pure survival mode. Everyone kept telling us to get through the first few months and we'd be alright, so with faith and trust we kept powering through.

One particular early morning toward the end of Lucy's colicky stint stands out in my mind. My wife and I had figured out our own little system of shared responsibility so that both of us would have a fighting chance at enjoying some shut-eye. Since I was working, my wife would handle any disruptions in the middle of the night, and then I'd get up early in the morning to attend to Lucy if needed before I headed out for the day. Most days she would get up between 4:30 and 5:00am, have a small bottle, and then knock back out. On this particular day, however, she decided to go off script.

I remember rocking her in my arms, assuming she would go back to sleep without a fight. At first, she played right along. Her eyes would close, and I'd feel the tension of her body loosening. I thought to myself, *"It's go time. Let's get this little girl down before she wakes back up…"* With the grace of a ninja, I attempted to place her back in her crib without jostling her. As soon as her back hit the mattress, her eyes opened, and crying ensued. I picked her back up and started the process again. A little rocking, a little swaying, and a little two-step for good measure. Just a little motion to guide her back to sleep. Once she dozed off again, I took my levels of grace to that of a ballerina and placed her back in her crib. Her eyes opened as quickly as they had the first time, bringing us both back to square one.

This song and dance played itself out a handful of times, and each time I'd find myself a little more frustrated.

I was frustrated that she wouldn't go back to sleep.

I was frustrated that I couldn't get her there (all ego, for sure).

I was frustrated that it was probably keeping my wife up despite it being her turn to rest.

I was frustrated that I was getting frustrated. I mean, how good a dad could I be if I was annoyed that my daughter couldn't get back to sleep?

Every time we had to start from scratch, more tension built up in my body. My loving fatherly sway was turning into a more aggressive jig, trying to get her to nod off. The emotion of frustration was bubbling underneath my skin, and I knew if she didn't get to sleep soon, it would be bad for everyone.

So, with a hint of shame and embarrassment after an hour of failed attempts, I sheepishly asked my wife if she could take over. Without judgment, she hopped out of bed and stepped in when I needed her most. I said thank you about a thousand times and went downstairs to collect myself.

I stood in our kitchen replaying the events that had just transpired, wrestling with my thoughts and emotions. There was a part of me that wanted to validate my frustrations because parenting can be hard at times. And there was another part of me that wanted to judge the hell out of the guy who was looking to justify his frustrations with his daughter. There was so much inner conflict that my head was spinning.

I took a deep breath to collect myself...*and then I fucking lost it.* I had a good, ugly cry alone in our kitchen. At first, I tried to fight it, but once the floodgates were opened, there was no closing them.

Looking back, it was one of the best experiences of my early days as a parent. Why? Because I set free months of pent-up emotion. I felt so much lighter once I let those emotions of anger, frustration, and pessimism run through me. As I said before, my wife and I were just trying to survive those first few months as parents given Lucy's colic. While in survival mode, I never stopped to let my emotions run through me. Instead, I bottled up the internal war of negative emotion and the guilt I felt for having them.

"Man, this is hard."

"Quit being a selfish prick; be grateful that you're blessed with this little girl."

"That was really aggravating."

"You're really going to complain right now? You should be ashamed."

Rather than accepting the way I was feeling and allowing myself to acknowledge those emotions, I kept trying to unfeel them. I kept trying to shame myself into feeling better about the situation. I knew that I was supposed to feel grateful that my wife and I were blessed with this silly little girl who was part me and part her, but the gap between how I "should" feel and how I actually felt was so wide that within it was created a storm of frustration, guilt, and shame that came pouring out on that early morning in the kitchen.

DON'T FEAR YOUR FEELINGS, EMBRACE THEM

There is no emotion that you "should" feel, only the one that you're currently experiencing. When we create expectations around how we're supposed to be feeling but deep down feel the opposite, that conflict wages a battle within that becomes hard to resolve. The longer we let that conflict stir and the longer that battle carries on, the worse we feel about ourselves, who we are, and our lives in general.

Our job as humans isn't only to feel the positive, uplifting emotions; it is to experience the full spectrum of emotions. All of them. Each one, from joy and bliss to grief and despair. The better you become at letting your emotions in and allowing them to flow through you, the easier it will become to navigate the tougher emotions that come your way.

Think about it for a second. When you find yourself staring down experiences in your life that might stimulate grief, frustration, or anger, you want to run the other way. You don't want those emotions to bring you down, so you pretend they're not there. You play defense and ignore them, even though they're right in front of you.

That defense is all based in fear.

You're scared of what it might mean if you feel sad. You're afraid of where your emotions might take you if you let your anger sink its teeth into you. You fear how dark it might get if you allow your grief to wash over you. The more defense you play, the scarier it gets. You make up stories in your head about all the bad things that will happen if you open yourself up to potential emotional pain.

So you keep those emotions at a distance. You push them away, petrified of what might happen if you let them be felt. It might feel safer. It might feel like the right thing to do to keep you sane. But with all that defense you're playing, there are two negative side effects that may not initially occur to you:

You're exhausted

The energy that you'll have to expend to keep unwanted emotions at a distance is more taxing than you may realize. You see this happen quite often when people are grieving the loss of a loved one. They work so hard to be strong during calling hours and the funeral, trying to put on a brave face for anyone who's come to pay their respects. With each interaction they have and every hour that passes, they grow more tired from playing it cool. And then, a song, a picture, or a memory hits their heart or their gut, causing a release of all of that sorrow and sadness that they've been holding onto. It's gut wrenching in the moment, but they feel lighter and more energized once they stop carrying around that emotional weight. The longer you fight off that emotional release, the more tiring it will become.

The less you allow yourself to feel the negative emotions, the less you'll be able to feel the good ones

Your ability to really feel your emotions and be in tune with that experience is a skill that you hone over time. If you close yourself off from allowing negative emotions to run their course, you run the risk of not having the capacity to be present within the many beautiful emotions we all want to enjoy. If you can't fully feel grief, you won't be able to really enjoy its polar opposite: joy. If you don't allow fear to run its course, your ability to deeply feel love will be tainted. To feel an emotion is to surrender to it. We all want to be wrapped up in love, joy, and bliss, but we only get to that place by practicing our ability to surrender to all emotions, not just the ones that feel good.

BE CONSCIOUS AND CURIOUS OF HOW YOU FEEL

Emotion is often baked into your being at a subconscious level, but that doesn't mean that you can't be conscious and curious about your feelings when they rise up. When you feel a bit off or you know something isn't quite right, instead of merely powering through that feeling, sit with it and try to work your way back to what may be at the root of the funk that you've found yourself in.

FEELING "OFF" ISN'T RANDOM. IT'S
THE RESULT OF BEING
EMOTIONALLY DISCONNECTED
FROM WHAT'S IN YOUR MIND.
DIG IN.

It might seem more normal or acceptable to brush it off and fight through it, but if there's an emotional weight on you, it's more efficient to do a little work to remove it than try to carry it with you through your day. Ask questions and try to retrace the mental, physical, and emotional steps that may have led you to where you are.

If you're sitting at your desk at work and you sense that something's bugging you but don't know what it is, do the work to find out. Was it something your boss said as you walked in? Was it the way you left the house? Were you in a rush and unable to say goodbye to your kids? Was it that coworker who *always* seems to get in the way of you getting your job done?

If you're upset with your spouse, get curious about why that is. Did they not follow through on a promise? Have they been distant lately? Have you been short with them and feel bad about it?

If you have a nagging frustration that shows up every time you call your mom, don't let that frustration linger. Figure out what caused it! Do you have latent resentment from something in your childhood? Did she say something judgmental about your house the last time you saw her? Did she not send you a birthday card for the first time in forty years?

No matter your situation, work your way back to the source of your emotional tension., Once you get there and identify the emotional baggage you've been carrying around, acknowledge and express it, and then let it go. Emotions are meant to be felt, not denied or kept at bay by your insistence on avoiding them. Once you release the emotions that may have previously felt heavy, you will feel freer to navigate toward the feelings you want to feel.

The morning when I struggled to get my daughter back to sleep, I tried to play defense against my emotions of frustration and anxiety. I didn't want to experience them, and truth be told, I felt guilty that they were showing up during a moment when I knew I should be giving off nothing but loving vibes to my little princess. The longer I boxed out those "bad" feelings, the more strongly they continued to build inside me.

But the moment I broke down in our kitchen, something amazing happened: **it all washed away.**

After about thirty seconds of truly experiencing and allowing my frustrations and guilt to run their course, I felt like a new man. As I let the feeling of frustration exit my body, I made way for love and appreciation. As I walked back into our room to re-claim my post as on-duty parent, my wife looked at me kind of funny. She sensed that I was struggling before and had an expression that said, *"Are you sure big guy? It looked like you were ready for a drink at 4:30 in the morning just a couple minutes ago..."*

But all of that tension was gone. I took my daughter back with a smile and a new sense of calm that I hadn't felt all morning. There's no way that I could have been helpful had I not had that moment in the kitchen. There's no way I could've gotten back to business with a smile on my face if I hadn't come face to face with some of the sadness that sat inside of me.

I had nothing but love and appreciation in my heart for our little girl. I was so grateful that she was ours; so grateful that I got to be her dad. But I wouldn't have been able to get there if I hadn't opened that emotional door and allowed myself to feel what so desperately needed to be felt.

Feel your feelings--or waste a ton of time and energy trying to claw your way to happiness. Let them in, let them go, and free yourself up to feel how you want to feel.

Chapter 13

What Facebook and Your Mind Have in Common

I'm going to go out on a limb and assume that you have Facebook. There are 7.7 billion people on the planet as of this writing, and Facebook is being used by one billion of those humans, so it's a decently strong limb that I'm walking out on here. Back when Facebook first began, it was little more than a cluster of status updates, in chronological order. The most recent thoughts of your Aunt Betty or cousin Jimmy were listed at the top, and the posts from your friends and family got older and older as you scrolled down.

And then, Facebook up and changed on us (and not for the last time). Instead of keeping the feed in order in terms of what was most recently posted, the book of faces started showing people more and more of the types of posts they often engaged with. If you shared and commented on inspirational memes, you'd find a bunch waiting for you every time you opened up the app. If you preferred to wage keyboard wars with those on the other side of the political aisle, more often than not, political drama would be at the top of your Facebook timeline. The more you favored something, the more Facebook took notice and gave you more of it.

It was weird at first, but people eventually got used to it. After all, the king of social media was providing more of what seemingly meant something to those on the website, so it wasn't too hard to mentally adapt to as a user.

You might think that this new feature was little more than a really neat form of new technology. *"That's crazy how it keeps showing me more videos of babies lip syncing! How does Facebook know me so well?!"* But all Facebook really did was tap into something old and primitive and bring it into a world of screens and status updates. **The behavior of your timeline became based simply on good ol' fashioned human behavior.**

We all get more of what we give our attention to.

When you spend your morning watching Fox News or CNN, you will walk out your front door and stumble into a world full of drama and politics.

When you spend your time and energy with positive people or positive thoughts, you will look out at the world and find something to celebrate with ease.

When you spend your days with people who are in great shape, you will somehow eat fewer donuts.

When you give a lot of energy to fear and anxiety, you will end up finding more things to be scared of and anxious about.

When you give your energy to something, you tend to find yourself in a vacuum of that something. Similar thoughts, people, and events will gravitate toward you and whatever it is that you spend most of your time with. You never really question it; you simply assume that everything that finds its way into your world just magically showed up for you. In a way, you'd be right. But there's also some science behind why you get more of what you focus on.

You have this little thing at the stem of your brain called the Reticular Activating System (RAS) that is responsible for bringing you more of what means something to you. With every moment that passes (like this one...and this one...and this one...), your senses are flooded with an ocean of stimuli. Sights, sounds, and a host of other things come at you with no mercy. The problem? You may be drowning in an ocean of stuff for your senses to sift through, but those senses of yours can only handle a river. Make that a pond. Eh, more like a puddle. The point is, you are not equipped to handle the world around you. You need to filter and simplify all of the input that's rushing into your brain so that you can make some sense of what the hell is going on.

That's where the RAS steps in to save the day.

Its main function is to cut out all the stuff around you that doesn't matter to you. It doesn't want to waste your time with things that you don't care about, so it only lets important information through. To avoid system overload, that RAS is pretty choosy about what it allows to slip through the cracks.

The best part about it? You have a say in this superpowered filter and its settings. Don't believe me? Let's try a little experiment.

Look around the room that you're currently sitting in. I want you to examine the space and identify anything that is the color blue. I don't care if it's royal, navy, or baby blue, just find anything that feels blueish to you. When you're done examining the room, bring your focus back to the book. Now, without looking back up at the room (and try to tell your peripheral vision to sit this one out), list off anything you saw that was...RED. Think hard. Give it your best shot. If you're in a room where you spend a lot of time, you probably have a memory of red objects. But otherwise, you're screwed. Why is that? It's because you informed your RAS that you were giving your attention to blue stuff, so it paid no mind to the red things around you. It's not that there isn't anything red in the room, it's that your RAS wanted to be spectacularly efficient in your search for anything blue. It was given a job, and it did it well.

This little demonstration was pretty small scale, though. It's cute that it could weed out colors that weren't blue, but what else can it do? Well, as it turns out, a lot. It can cut out beliefs that don't match yours, thoughts that you don't agree with, and people who don't align with who you're choosing to be. But as you've seen in our little experiment, you get to have a say. You can set the tone for what comes in and what stays out of your awareness.

With that in mind, take a minute to think about what kind of people you find yourself with the most, what ideologies seem to swarm your life, and what thoughts or beliefs you tend to resonate with. At some point, you told your RAS—whether you knew it or not—that that was the experience you wanted to have. Those were the things that you wanted to allow into your life.

The beautiful part of this is that you now have the power to decide to filter in something different, if you so choose. You get to choose what you focus on and filter out. If you decide that you want to be surrounded by more love in your life, somehow the people who exude hate will seem to fall by the wayside. If you decide that you want to get in shape, you'll miraculously see fewer ads for McDonald's and more for your local gym. If you decide that you want to be rich, you'll find more and more examples of wealth in your life.

It's a conscious choice that you must make, and with a little intentional practice of that conscious thought, your RAS will update to its new settings.

YOUR VIBE ATTRACTS YOUR TRIBE (AND EVERYTHING ELSE)

There's a little caveat to the whole idea of rewiring your RAS in your favor. You can say you want something, decide you desire something, and choose a different focus for your life...but if your energy is in opposition to those shifts, you're going to go nowhere fast.

For instance, let's say that you decide that you want to make more money and start living a more abundant life. Knowing that you have a say in what you give your attention to—which will then allow you to see more and more of that thing you desire—you start thinking about money, wealth, and all the fun stuff you'll get to do with your money. You start visualizing what it would be like to go on vacation on a whim. You start dreaming about what charities you could give back to with the cashflow you're bringing in. You really start putting some momentum behind your desire for more moolah.

But after a couple weeks of doing this, you hear that a girl you went to college with just won the lottery and had millions and millions of dollars fall right into her lap. You roll your eyes, begin to sulk, and let the words, "Must be nice..." roll off your tongue.

You keep thinking about money and how much you'd like to have more, but you can't help but feel the tinge of jealousy toward your old college friend. You resent her for stumbling into a buttload of cash when *you* were the one who was trying to get the Universe's attention, screaming into your megaphone, "I WANT MORE MONEY!"

The thing is, you were on the right track by attempting to reprogram your RAS for bigger and better things, but your sarcastic, jealous vibe about your friend's newfound wealth derailed your reprogramming mission. You may have heard the phrase "thoughts make things" before. To a certain extent, that's true. The more conscious thought you funnel toward what you want in life, the higher your probability of attaining what you desire. But the key ingredient that most people miss in the mix of this concept is that your energy and vibration *have* to match the level of the thought that you're thinking.

If you're all about making more money, and then find yourself frustrated by your friend's windfall of wealth, your inner annoyance is in conflict with all the thoughts you've been thinking about cranking up your cash flow. While your thoughts are living in the world of abundance, your energy is putting off a vibe of scarcity. It's like trying to run a race with your shoes tied together; you might be able to move things forward, but you're bound to trip due to all the knots (read: nots) you've tied yourself up in.

This conflict between thought and energy is what keeps so many people feeling stuck and defeated as they give their all to making the most of their lives. Whether you're striving toward more money, better relationships, a banging bod, or a promotion at work, this civil war between positive intentions and negative vibes will make it nearly impossible to make any progress.

So, as you look to reframe your thoughts and give attention to what you desire, be sure to stay conscious of how you're feeling about other people having what you want.

If you want to lose twenty pounds and Tonya at work just dropped a ton of weight by cleaning up her diet, try to avoid spiraling into a place of jealousy and resentment. Rather than gossiping about how she starved herself to achieve her goals, celebrate her hard work and ask her how she did it. If you want what she has created for yourself, reacting to her progress with hostility will simply show the Universe that you don't really want what you keep saying you do.

If you want to find the woman of your dreams, don't downplay your buddy's new flame, giving him a hard time for not hanging out with the boys. That type of energy makes you feel conflicted, causing you to hesitate when *you* meet your lady love because you don't want to experience the same relationship-shaming you just dished out.

You know the good ol' golden rule, right? "Do unto others as you would have them do unto you." Treating others the way you want to be treated is a great start, but to take this most golden rule to another level, give energy as you wish to have it given to you. If you want to be celebrated when you reached your version of success, celebrate others when they reach similar milestones. Just because someone else got a promotion, lost some weight, or found The One doesn't mean that those things aren't available to you. In fact, the more you throw shade in their direction for their achievements, the less likely it will be that you create similar success in your own life.

When broke people hate on rich people, they're just acknowledging what they don't have, signaling to their RAS that they want to focus more on their lack of wealth. Ouch.

When single people talk shit about married people, they're just highlighting that committed relationships are negative in some way. If those single people truly desire to find love, they're only making it harder by operating through a negative "ball and chain" filter.

When overweight people look down on skinny people while grubbing on a bucket of chicken, they're making it nearly impossible to put that deep-fried goodness down and get to the gym. If they want to stay in that KFC-loving state, then all is well. But if they want to drop some weight and get back into their "goal jeans," they have to celebrate the people who are in shape and get their energy from a place that honors those who are healthy.

Your conscious thoughts and energy are the compass that your body and mind will follow. If you are engaging with people who are negative, your world will be overwhelmed with that negativity. If you resent people who have what you want, the Universe will start resenting you and your goals. If you focus your attention on what you need to fix about yourself or what you need to find to be happy, you'll experience more evidence of how broken you are and how lost you've been.

You are a conscious creator. You have the ability to steer your time, energy, and attention toward whatever you desire. The more you harness your power to choose where you put your focus in life, the more you will create *exactly* what you want.

SCARCITY VS. ABUNDANCE: WHY YOU'RE REALLY HATING ON OTHER PEOPLE'S SUCCESS

You've now seen why it's important to direct your attention toward things you desire and how to harness the power of your own biology and your RAS. Along with that, you now have a sense of why it's important to keep your energy and emotions in line with the things, people, and achievements that you really, really want—a.k.a. quit being a douche to people who already have what you have your heart and mind set on. But let's dive a little deeper on *why* you are hating on those who have what you want in the first place. Once you become aware of what's at the core of that jealousy and resentment, it'll be easier to sidestep that nonsense and celebrate your face off with anyone raking in the loot, sculpting the perfect body, or married to their soulmate.

You're not a bad person if you sarcastically say, "I'm so happy for you!" while flipping the bird behind your back to those you envy. You're simply imprisoned by a scarcity mindset. You are viewing their success through a lens of all that you're lacking in life, putting your focus on how you lost rather than honoring their wins. You believe that if your friend, cousin, or coworker sniffs some success, there is less success for you to have.

> IN ORDER FOR YOU TO CREATE MORE IN YOUR LIFE THAN YOU CURRENTLY HAVE, YOU HAVE TO BELIEVE THAT THERE'S MORE AVAILABLE TO YOU. IF YOU LIVE IN SCARCITY, THIS BECOMES FRUSTRATINGLY IMPOSSIBLE.

That whole scarcity thing, though? Yeah, it's all my fault. Well, not exactly. But as a math teacher, I feel that I should shoulder some of the blame.

Think about the way you learned about fractions when you were younger. There's a pretty good chance that the introduction was made with a visual of, a discussion of, or the actual use of a pie of some kind. Whether the pie was in the form of pizza or pumpkin, teachers have forever relied on those circles of deliciousness to communicate the concept of fractions to little kids. The pie starts off as a whole, then gets cut and divided up into smaller portions so everyone can see what one half or one third of a whole would look like.

As your idea of fractions evolved, your teacher may have asked you some critical thinking questions like, "If Johnny cuts the pie into eight even pieces, gives two pieces to Jimmy and then three pieces to Jenny, how many pieces will he get to have?" How am I doing so far? Is my script spot on?

You'd do a little mental math, scouring your brain to figure out how much of the pie was left over for Johnny (the answer is three pieces, for those keeping score). In terms of teaching the subject of fractions, this method is pretty solid. But, unfortunately, this classic approach to fractions does some long-term damage when it comes to life lessons.

The premise in all of this is that you're trying to figure out how much of the pie is left for Johnny to scrape up from that one tin. What you don't consider in your attempt to please your teacher and get the answer right is that the pie in question isn't the only pie that exists in the world. Johnny doesn't have to settle for just three pieces of pizza or pumpkin pie if he doesn't want to. He can order another pie and have it all to himself if he desires.

You've been programmed to fill in the blanks, look for the scraps, and analyze what's left in the pie. You are trained in finding what's left over, which inherently forces you to figure out how much of the pie has been taken away. Your mind has been wired to look for scarcity.

Is it a little dramatic to blame whoever taught you about fractions for your lack of an abundance mindset? For sure. But does it highlight why you feel a little tightness in your chest when your buddy gets a $10,000 raise and you haven't? You bet.

Living your life filtered through a scarcity mindset causes you to think that there isn't enough to go around. If your sibling finds love, that takes away from the pool of people you get to choose from. If your buddy gets that raise, there's now less money available for you to get a raise as well. If your neighbor wins a vacation of a lifetime, you immediately focus on the fact that you didn't win that trip. Having a scarcity mindset is forever looking at the world as one pie, and if anyone else takes a piece away from that pie, you cry yourself to sleep at night thinking about how much smaller your piece of the pie keeps getting.

But, again, there isn't only one pie. There's an infinite number of them. You've just been so stuck in fraction mode, splitting up one pie amongst all of the humans around you, that you freak the hell out if anyone advances in any area of life.

Just because someone else started a business and is making some money doesn't mean that you can't, too. On an average day, there are $5 trillion dollars being spent and exchanged around the world. That means there is always money to be made, and you don't have to worry or stress if someone else has found a way to make some. There's plenty available to you.

Just because your buddy found his soulmate doesn't mean that you can't, too. Again, there are roughly 7.7 billion humans alive right now. That doesn't exactly sound like a shortage that should threaten your ability to find a guy or girl you'd like to kick it with for eternity. Cheer up, buttercup.

When you read numbers like five trillion and 7.7 billion, I hope that it reminds you that the amount of opportunity for you and everything that you're looking to accomplish is pretty much limitless. You DO NOT need to worry about how small your slice of the pie is getting if other people take their fair share. The pie is freakin' ginormous, dammit.

Seeing the world and the crazy amount of opportunity that's out there through a lens that acknowledges all the billions and trillions of things available to you allows you to operate from a place of abundance. When you live abundantly, you don't need to stress and worry that you're getting gypped out of the life that you desire because Susie down the street just made her first million, met the man of her dreams, or just got back from her yearly trip to Fiji. You can have everything Susie has, because all of the same things are available to you.

Your mind can't even fathom the number of things that you can acquire or accomplish in this life of yours, so don't try to fry your brain trying to rationally figure it all out right now. Just trust and believe that the only limits that you have are the ones that you've agreed to. The amount of opportunity that's out there and ready for you to seize is just a hair away from infinite.

There's no reason to resent anyone for their success because now you consciously know that you can have what they have. Screw it, you can have something better than that. You get to have your own version of greatness, and there's very little holding you back aside from your belief that you can't make it happen. So choose to put down the mental baggage that's been weighing you down, and open yourself up to the limitless opportunity that you're allowed to take advantage of.

When you choose to focus on that, your world will open up in ways you can't even imagine.

Chapter 14

Start with...Who

When I first was motivated to improve my station in life, reading books and listening to podcasts at a record pace, I was on a desperate mission to figure out **what** I had to do to amplify my life. I'd take notes, do exercises, and attempt any life hack that I discovered in hopes that trying anything and everything would somehow create change in my life. For a while there, I cranked things up a notch. I was meditating consistently, exercising more regularly than ever, and had begun making money on the side as a freelance writer. I got a real taste for what change and transformation felt like and became hooked to the high of seeing what else I could do to continue to move everything forward.

Then I came across an amazing book by Simon Sinek titled *Start With Why*. I had spent a year or so tirelessly chasing **what** I should be doing differently that I hadn't really dug deeply into **why** I was doing it in the first place. Don't get me wrong; I wasn't flailing about aimlessly, taking a whole bunch of action without a purpose in mind. I knew in my heart that the reason behind everything that I was trying to create was my wife and future family. But Sinek's book forced me to look at that a little bit deeper, a few layers below the surface of what I assumed was the reason I wanted to keep improving. That led me down a rabbit hole that introduced me to the legacy I wanted to create, the people I wanted to impact, and the dent I wanted to leave in the world. My family was at the core of my mission, but I wanted the love that I had for them to reverberate out to anyone who was looking to be inspired by that kind of love rather than live a monotonous life filled with fear.

As my *why* grew stronger and got deeper, I opened up my heart and soul to the world of coaching. I wanted to create a ripple effect of positivity and empower people to shift their life out of a state of mediocrity. I had a feeling that simply posting inspiring posts on Facebook or on my blog wasn't going to leave too big of a mark. I needed to connect with people one-on-one to make the difference I aspired to see. I stumbled out of the gate in my business, but since I was deeply connected to why I wanted to make it happen, I figured it was only a matter of time until I was changing the world. I onboarded some clients, had an amazing time providing them with whatever tools and methods I had in my arsenal, and then…

Nothing.

After building a ton of momentum toward a life I was excited by, things sort of fell flat. No more clients, not a ton of freelance writing gigs, and a whole lot of questioning myself and what I did wrong to fall into such a lull.

"Are my prices too high?"

"Am I not any good at this whole coaching thing?"

"Is my writing not valuable anymore?"

"Do I not know words, let alone have the best words?"

A level of self-doubt that I previously thought I had escaped crept back into my life just when I thought I was figuring it all out. Then I came across the following quote:

> *"Don't think **of** your ideal, think **from** it. It is only the ideals **from** which you think that are ever realized."*
> —Neville Goddard

Now, Neville's stuff can get a little heady at times, so let me break this one down, at least the way it resonated with me.

We all have a sense of what our ideal life looks like. Whether you have dreams of traveling the world, growing old with your partner, stacking up loads of cash, or all of the above, you probably have a rough idea of how it will go down. Whether you catch yourself daydreaming in the middle of your workday or intentionally plot out what you desire on a daily or weekly basis, I'd bet good money that there's a corner of your mind with a sign hanging over it that says "My Ideal Life."

But what many of us end up doing is idealizing our future and thinking of it from time to time rather than thinking from it consistently. We think of how cool it would be to make a million bucks or fly first class to Fiji to see if their water is really $3 better per bottle than any other water in the world. We dream of the wedding day for the record books and the day our kids ship off to college. We think *of* our ideal future, but we rarely step into that vision and live our lives *from* it.

When we think *of* that dream life, we are simply observing it. We are viewing it like a movie on a screen; a movie that, from our perspective, is fictional. The events are manufactured stories that live off in the future somewhere. It doesn't feel real to us because, from where we stand, it isn't.

When we think *from* that dream life, we are living in it in real time. We are stepping into the shoes of our future selves--hearing what they hear, feeling what they feel, smelling what they smell. We are getting in touch with what it's like to be that person, rather than just considering the possibility of arriving there someday.

The latter gives us the perspective that our desires have already been realized, giving us an idea of **who** we are going to be and how we will have to operate to make it happen. It offers certainty and a clear picture of the identity that's required to get the job done. The former just supplies us with a narrative of how cool it would be if our desires were to come to pass. It keeps us separate from the identity of who that person is, only supplying us with hopeful information of what could be.

When we think *from* the perspective of our dream life, we get to experience the energy and identity that caused and created all the amazing things that were once simply a vision. It fills in all the blanks in terms of who we have to become. Thinking *of* our dream life only gives us a picture, but it doesn't give us the detail of what made the picture come to life.

So, how did this quote change the trajectory of my life—and possibly, in this moment, yours? It woke me up to how often I was thinking *of* the life I wanted to create and almost never thinking *from* it. I was stuck and frustrated with my progress because I had maxed out the amount of growth I could muster while viewing my future as something that was off in the distance. I had read enough books to figure out **what** habits would get me to a new level of life. I had gone deep into **why** my ambitions meant something to me.

But when I took Neville's advice and started using my imagination to view my goals from the place where they were already accomplished, I began to get a sense of **who** I needed to become.

I could feel his vibe. I felt his swagger, confidence, and certainty in my bones. And once I decided to step into that identity, the whole game changed. I raised my coaching rates because I knew what I was truly worth. I started showing up with more presence for my family because my new identity made that non-negotiable. I started asking for (and receiving) more for any freelance writing jobs I was hired for. And to be quite honest, I started writing this book. When I stepped into the shoes of Future Nick, I looked around and saw books with his name on the cover. I knew it was time to share my message and be open with my journey, so to the keyboard I came. Everything started to click in ways it hadn't before. And it was all because I figured out **who** I needed to be.

WHO ARE YOU?

When you know who you are, everything else gets easier. If you identify as a vegetarian, you don't eat meat. If I go out to eat with you, you don't spend twenty minutes sifting through the burger options or salivating over the different cuts of steak they have. You ignore that part of the menu and hone in on what fits with your identity. Here I am feeling bad for you because you don't get to enjoy all the tasty meat that I love, but you probably feel bad for me because I can't decide between the eight different options that all sound amazing to me.

Having a firm identity simplifies your life because it cuts out all the nonsense. When you know who you are, you also know with certainty who you are not. People who don't have a strong sense of identity get all wishy washy when it comes to making decisions. Those who are clear about the way they identify themselves get right to the point. Things are either your jam or they're not. If you're a vegetarian, you don't like meat. If you're a Yankees fan, you never root for the Red Sox. If you're a republican, you probably didn't like Obama. If you're a human, you probably aren't a huge fan of Trump. It's black and white. After typing the last sentence, I realize its odd juxtaposition after my short political tangent, but it also made me laugh. So I'm not deleting it.

To get back to the point, though, your identity— who you believe yourself to be—is the compass of your life. When push comes to shove, it will decide what you do, how you think, and what you believe. So, having a conscious awareness of what your identity is—and to Neville's point, what it will be when you've realized your desires—will alter the course of your life.

> MAKING A DECISION ON WHO YOU
> WANT TO BECOME MAY SOUND
> LESS SEXY THAN A STEP-BY-STEP
> ROADMAP TO SUCCESS, BUT YOUR
> DIRECTION IN LIFE AND ALL THE
> PLANS THAT COME WITH IT CAN
> ONLY BE DECIDED THROUGH THE
> IDENTITY OF THE PERSON AT THE
> WHEEL.

Who is it that you hope to become? Step into their shoes and feel into what a day in their life is really like. What do they do on a daily basis? Are they getting up early or sleeping in? Are they hitting the gym today or waiting until Monday to start? Are they loving with an open heart or staying guarded so they don't get hurt? Are they waiting for other people to give them permission to pursue what they desire or are they getting after it without the approval of other humans? Are they living with courage or living in fear?

Decide right now who you are, and compare that to the identity of the human that you're aiming to actualize. Do you notice a gap between the two versions of yourself? Minimize that gap by taking ownership of the identity from your desired state of life. How much physical evidence do you need in front of you to fully lean into the identity that you desire to step into? None. The answer is none. You don't need an amazing marriage to be loving. You don't need a huge bank account to be generous. You don't need a huge business to be worthy. There are no requirements for a state of being.

Just decide to be that person, and do it now. Practice their way of life and expect that what they have will soon be yours. Create a new identity, and become the **who** that your dream life requires. The what, the why, the how, the when...they will all figure themselves out once your identity is aligned with the life you would love to live. Be that person today.

Chapter 15

Life is Short But Sweet for Certain

As mere words, "life" and "death" don't measure up to the depth of their concepts. We toss them around casually in conversation, but no one ever really feels the weight of them until either one is thrust upon them. The summer of 2017 taught me a lot about both life and death, as I experienced them both in a way that I never had previously.

On July 3rd, I came home from a long day of golf in need of a nap. After what most would consider a mediocre round of golf—ironic, I know—I walked in the door and laid down on the couch, ready to catch some shut-eye. What I didn't know was that I wouldn't need that nap after all; my wife had some news that was sure to give me a second wind. As my eyes began to close, she snuck an object into my foggy line of vision. With my eyelids begging me to close up shop, I squinted one last time to try and make out what she was trying to show me.

PREGNANT. Yeah, no chance of me sleeping at that point.

My body cooked up quite the brew of emotion that sucker punched me right out of my mid-afternoon drowsy state. I was excited, nervous, overjoyed, and scared as hell all in one moment. I was going to be a dad! As much as I wanted to jump for joy, I also wanted to hyperventilate. After living in a one-bedroom apartment for three years, we had just moved into a new townhouse, ready for a fresh start. Boy, did we get one. Throughout the rest of that summer, we went to various doctor appointments to be sure all things were moving in the right direction. Thankfully, all was well in the womb, and our little girl, Lucy, was making herself right at home.

Back where I grew up, my grandma was visiting her doctors quite a bit as well. Her visits were less about creating life and more about preserving what little life she had left. My grandma had always been a smoker. Her house always had that dingy, pack-a-day scent baked into the carpet that hit your nose as soon as you walked in. Years and years of lighting up had slowly deteriorated her lungs and her ability to breathe, to the point that she needed to be hooked up to an oxygen tank most of the day just to get by.

In early August, I got word that she had been admitted to the hospital. With her lungs as bad as they were, any time she came down with a cold she ended up there, so it wasn't terribly odd that she was there again. Since I hadn't seen her in a while, I wanted to drive out to visit her in the hospital and try to lift her spirits. The running joke in my family is that she favored me in comparison to her other grandkids, mainly because I reminded her of my dad. My old man was her baby and her far and away favorite, so as his firstborn son, I got the favoritism hand-me-downs. I figured an impromptu visit from her favorite grandson couldn't hurt, right?

Before I hopped in the car to make the short trek to my hometown, I found a copy of one of the first ultrasounds we had experienced so I could surprise my grandma with the good news. At that point, we hadn't told many people outside of our immediate families and close friends, so I was excited to let her in on our little secret. I tucked the ultrasound picture into a "get well soon" card and hit the open road.

When I got into town, I headed over to the hospital with my parents and my brother, anxious to see how my grandma was doing. We walked in and gave our hugs, then sat down to chat and see how she'd been feeling. After a bit of catching up, I presented my surprise to her with butterflies in my stomach. She opened it and read the card, trying to process what she was looking at. After she understood that Christina and I were going to be having a baby, she teared up and rejoiced in the good news. My grandma was one tough cookie, so to see her be overwhelmed with emotion—especially given her state of physical health—was really a beautiful moment. The rest of our visit was spent talking about what was to come of this little baby growing inside of my wife's belly. I'd say we were there for an hour or two before my grandma needed some rest. As we headed out, I told her I loved her and gave a little kiss on the cheek. She returned the "I love you" and said congratulations one more time.

That was the last time I ever saw my grandma alive.

That visit to the hospital put life and death in the same room for me. They were no longer merely words strung together with four or five letters but an experience. On one hand, we celebrated what would eventually become my daughter. On the other, that hospital visit marked the very last time I got to spend time with my grandma.

Over the next month or so, there were tears of all kinds as we laid my grandma to rest, then just a few weeks later found out we were having a girl. We lost the eldest lady in our family and quickly found out that we would be blessed with a little lady to step right into the void that my grandma's death created.

That summer allowed me to bear witness to life and death. It gave me perspective that I hadn't had prior, and with that perspective I learned two very important things in real time:

Death is real and life is rare.

DEATH IS REAL

You and I are not naive enough to think that death is fictional, but we all observe it sort of like we view school shootings or starving kids in Africa. We think, *"That's really sad, but that would never happen to me."* It's sort of like a distant sympathy, something that saddens you, but you can't truly understand it because it doesn't really hit home. Until it does.

Death doesn't play favorites. It doesn't excuse anyone. Everyone you know will one day stand face-to-face with it, including you.

I'm not saying all of this to cast a morbid tone over the rest of this book, it's just that I need you to understand that you have a limited amount of time here. You have a shot clock whether you like it or not. For some people, that's scary as hell. For me, seeing my grandma pass on after years of knowing her and loving her did the opposite.

It gave me a front row seat to mortality and inspired me to make the most of the moments I have left. I'm thirty years old. Odds are good that I have millions of moments left to live, but none of them are guaranteed. Whether I'm alive for another seventy years or get hit by a bus tomorrow, her passing reminded me that I need to truly live until my time comes.

Don't let death scare you. It's a fact of life, just like gravity. Being afraid of either won't make them non-existent, but being aware of them will allow you to live optimally.

You don't spend every day trying to avoid gravity, do you? It's not a soul-sucking presence that doesn't allow you to live fully, right? Of course not. You just avoid jumping off buildings or hopping out of an airplane without a parachute and carry on without a worry in the world. Similar to gravity, death just is. It exists. There's no way around it. But it doesn't have to cripple you with fear. Just acknowledge that it exists, avoid the obvious traps that might have you succumb to it—ironically, jumping off a building or out of an airplane sans parachute also happen to be things to avoid here—and wake up each day cherishing the time that you have left.

Start that business.

Write that book.

Ask that girl out.

Have (or adopt) that kid.

Learn to play the guitar.

Travel.

Forgive your ex, your mom, or your former best friend.

You're running on borrowed time here, my friend. You don't get another shot at this thing. At some point, it's all going to end. Moving past mediocre requires that you acknowledge your certain death and use it to propel you out of the minutiae of average that you've been living in.

Do you really want to lie on your deathbed bearing the weight of regret? I didn't think so. Get off your couch and start living the life you truly desire. The probability of you dying is 100 percent. The probability of you truly being alive, though, is much, much smaller.

LIFE IS RARE

I've heard it said that the probability of us being born is approximately 1 in 400 trillion. You know how lucky you feel when the Roulette wheel stops at the only number you decided to play? The chances of that happening are one in thirty-seven. You represent the one shot in 400 trillion opportunities that came to life. Winning a load of money on the Roulette table seems like a sure thing when you look at it next to the odds of you being alive.

We've normalized the idea of being here so much that we don't even realize how lucky we are to be alive. Of all the things you've ever taken for granted, I'm sure this is the biggest one. The probability that your parents met, conceived you, and successfully brought you into the world is just one small piece of the puzzle. There are plenty of other variables at play, going back generations and generations. All you need to know is that your unique self, strutting your stuff every single day is a goddamn miracle. You're not special only because it's just a nice thing to say to someone. You're special because, mathematically, it doesn't make sense that you're here.

My grandma made the concept of death very real to me. My daughter did the same for the concept of life. As Lucy's due date approached, I couldn't help but think about what a miracle she was. This little human was about to move out of the home that she made for herself in the womb and come to be a permanent part of my life. Do you know how crazy it is to stare at something knowing that they are scientifically 50 percent you? Like, I'm one whole person over here, but my daughter is still half me in some way. I still can't quite wrap my head around that one.

My daughter's existence, my existence, and your existence are all so unique and rare that it would be a crime to waste this one opportunity we have. Imagine yourself in a line with 399,999,999,999,999 other people and finding out that they drew your name from the hat. Because that's pretty much what happened.

Remain conscious of how certain death is and how unbelievably remarkable it is to be alive. Use both as a reminder that you shouldn't waste years of your life doing things that you hate doing. Mediocrity is a choice, and by choosing it, you're wasting an incredible opportunity to live this one life you have to its fullest.

Choose joy.

Choose love.

Choose happiness.

Choose excitement.

Choose adventure.

You don't want to get to the end of this few-and-far-between experience and wish you got more out of it. I don't want that for you, either.

CONCLUSION

Leave a Little Room for Magic

Well, there you have it. I hope that as I've poured myself into this project, you've taken away some insights from the musings of my mind, and in turn, opened yours up to the infinite possibilities you have to live an amazing life.

Before I leave you, though, I want to remind you to leave yourself open to magic and miracles as you continue your path of self-improvement and personal growth. When you begin to honor your worth and take care of yourself, the Universe tends to throw some bonus prizes your way. Keep your eye out for them.

The truth is that I don't have it all figured out, and neither does anyone else. This book is intended to provide you with a good foundation with which to start your new story, but the minor details that will make your story compelling and awe inspiring will probably be gifted to you along the way. You won't be able to plan for them. You won't see them coming. But trust me, when you start to arrange your life around a meaningful and non-mediocre narrative, the best plot lines will tend to fall into your lap.

I'll end where all of this began for me. Got time for one more story?

It was a hot summer night in June 2013, and I had plans of heading out with some good friends of mine. I had just moved back in with my parents after breaking up with my ex-girlfriend, bringing all of my stuff home from the place that we shared. A night out with the boys was what I needed to shake the funk I was feeling. I felt good about the breakup overall, as it was a long time coming, but moving back home and starting over was disorienting. Luckily, the guys were prepared to help me clear my head.

We didn't have anything out of the ordinary in mind. The plan was to hit the bars about ten minutes away from my buddy's house the way we normally would and mingle with any familiar faces we came across. The night started off normally, but there wasn't much really going on. In an attempt to mix it up, we started brainstorming about what we could do to make the night more interesting. We ended up deciding to head out to Buffalo for the night—about thirty to forty minutes away from where we were—

where a girl who one of my friends was dating happened to be gallivanting with her friends. We hopped in a vehicle and hit the road with hopes that things would get more interesting at our new location.

A couple hours earlier, my now-wife, Christina, was mulling over what she was going to do that night. She didn't want to do the same old thing she'd been doing every Friday night out in Rochester, NY, so with some encouragement from her sister and the help of a friend who was down for a spontaneous adventure, she hopped in the car and headed out of town. They weren't just going to the next town over, though. They were hitting the highway and heading an hour and a half west until they arrived right where my buddies and I were: Buffalo.

It was 3:30 am and the guys and I were ready to head home after closing down the night at Skybar, a rooftop spot that was perfect for summer nights like that one. We headed toward the elevator that would take us down to the ground floor, knowing we were about to get the sardine treatment along with all the others who were ready to call it a night.

As we shuffled into that sweat box of an elevator, my friend, Travis, tried one last pickup line for the night when he saw the outfit of one of the girls we were huddled next to. "Hey, I like your dress!" To my surprise, the attempt didn't bomb, and he and the girl struck up a conversation. As we rode the elevator down, I noticed that the girl in the dress was with a friend. Attempting to help my friend out and step in as his wingman, I introduced myself to her. We shared a couple of smiles, some witty banter, and before we knew it, we had arrived at the elevator's destination. We exchanged numbers and went our separate ways for the night.

I knew that there was chemistry there. What I didn't know was that I had just met my wife.

If any part of that night would have played out differently, I wouldn't be who I am or where I am today. Meeting my wife introduced me to magic, miracles, and a belief in things that can't be planned for or explained. If I would've taken the next elevator, I would've missed her. If I would've stayed home that night, we wouldn't have ever met. Hell, if I had done everything the exact same way but taken the stairs instead of the elevator, I'd be miles down a different path right now.

I could have read every last personal development book, listened to every podcast, and watched every damn Tony Robbins video on YouTube in order to build a perfect life with intention. But there's nothing I could've done to prepare myself for that chance meeting with my wife. No one's giving out "just keep riding elevators" as relationship advice (to my knowledge), so there's no way I could've meticulously planned such an encounter.

The point is, you need to leave yourself open to the magic that is ready to enter your life. You can set goals, plan your days, and execute with intention, but leave some room for the Universe to gift you some miracles in the process.

When you make the choice to actively move past mediocrity in your life, the Universe gets put on notice. It knows that you mean business and are ready for some changes. As you continue to show commitment to yourself and your greater good, it will honor your commitments and start chucking gifts in your direction. You just have to be ready to receive them.

I broke up with my ex-girlfriend because I knew I was worthy and deserving of more than that relationship was giving me. That commitment to myself opened up my world to the magic that I was owed.

I met Christina a month later.

I moved in with her a year later.

I proposed just a month after moving in.

That chance meeting in an elevator has been my life's biggest blessing. But there's no way I could've planned it. All I did was make a decision that was in my best interest and trusted that everything was going to be okay. I broke it off with the girl I was dating and had faith that things would fall into place. I put myself in a position to welcome magic into my life, and on that night in June at about 3:30 in the morning, a miracle showed up out of nowhere.

Everything that I laid out for you in these pages has been learned through a few years of digging deep into my own soul, the brains of smarter people who came before me, and the minds of the people I work with. The information, methods, and tools here are simply the effects of something I did well before this moment I'm in as I write this sentence.

The cause of those effects? Me betting on myself, leaving a relationship that didn't serve me, and trusting that things would work out in my favor.

I had to go first, and so do you. Let the world know that you're ready for the next level of your life, and be open to what comes your way as you move forward.

Never stop moving past mediocre.

—Nick

ACKNOWLEDGMENTS

Behind marrying my wife and becoming a father to our daughter, Lucy, getting this book written and published probably takes the bronze medal on the podium of my greatest and most pride-inducing accomplishments. Seeing my name on the cover of this book was a big deal for me, but what means a great deal more is that you took the time to read it. So to you, the reader, I have a ton of gratitude. Thank you for investing your time, money, and energy in my (hopefully) amusing stories and my insights along the way. You're awesome!

In addition to you people who have read, highlighted, and folded some pages over to return to later, there are a few specific people who deserve their time in the spotlight as well.

To my amazing wife, Christina: thank you so much for being you. This book never would have gotten written if it weren't for your love and support. From the journey I've had in this world of personal development to the actual process of writing this book, you have been one hell of a cheerleader. So, thank you, my love.

To my little girl, Lucy: thank you for being a constant reminder of love, joy, and laughter for your mom and me. I have no idea when you'll read this book or find your way to the acknowledgment section to find your name. By then you will likely have a brother, a sister, or both. But just know that becoming a father was one of the greatest gifts I've ever received. It's made me a better man and gave this book so much more depth.

To my parents: thank you for showing me what love and family were supposed to look like as a kid. When Christina came waltzing into my life, pursuing her and our life together was the easiest decision I've ever made because I knew that she was my best shot of capturing that kind of marriage for myself.

To my sister, Brittany: thank you for showing me what hard work looked like growing up. I know I was a bit of a slacker, but I admired your effort in the classroom and in life.

To my brother, Jeff: thank you for showing me what it looks like to chase your passions in life. I fell in love with writing similar to the way you fell for baton twirling back in the day. Watching you tirelessly show up for what you love and become third in the world at something you enjoy was a hell of a sight to see.

To my friends: thank you for keeping me humble, gentlemen. This book could become a New York Times Bestseller and I know that you would still treat me like the Nick you met ten to fifteen years ago. And I appreciate the hell out of you for it.

To my coaches and mentors: each one of you have had a major impact on the creation of this book. Tommy Baker, working with you allowed me to see what was truly possible for me. Preston Pugmire, it was within a coaching conversation with you that I finally said, "I'm going to be an author, dammit!" And here we are. Nick Tillia, I have never felt more whole and complete in delivering my message in my own voice since working with you. That right there is a beautiful feeling, so thank you. You guys are all amazing and I'm honored to have been in your energy.

To the team that brought this book to life in a very real way: thank you! Elizabeth Lyons, having you on my side to edit and format this thing was such a gift to me. Chris and Debbie Byrnes, this cover is amazing; you guys really knocked it out of the park.

And finally, I want to thank Nick Matiash from a couple years ago. It was he who had the itch to deliver an inspiring message to the world and made the frightening decision to step into the unknown and figure out how. I'm just sitting here riding the momentum of everything he started. So thanks for your courage, Nick. You're the man.

ABOUT THE AUTHOR

Nick Matiash is a husband, father, men's life coach, high school teacher, content creator, and (now) published author. He is the owner and operator of Moving Past Mediocre, the platform he created to lead people to their version of success in mind, body, and soul. Nick lives in Webster, New York, with his wife and daughter.

www.movingpastmediocre.com

facebook.com/nickmatiashMPM

instagram.com/nick_movingpastmediocre

Made in the USA
San Bernardino, CA
10 July 2019